RENOIR

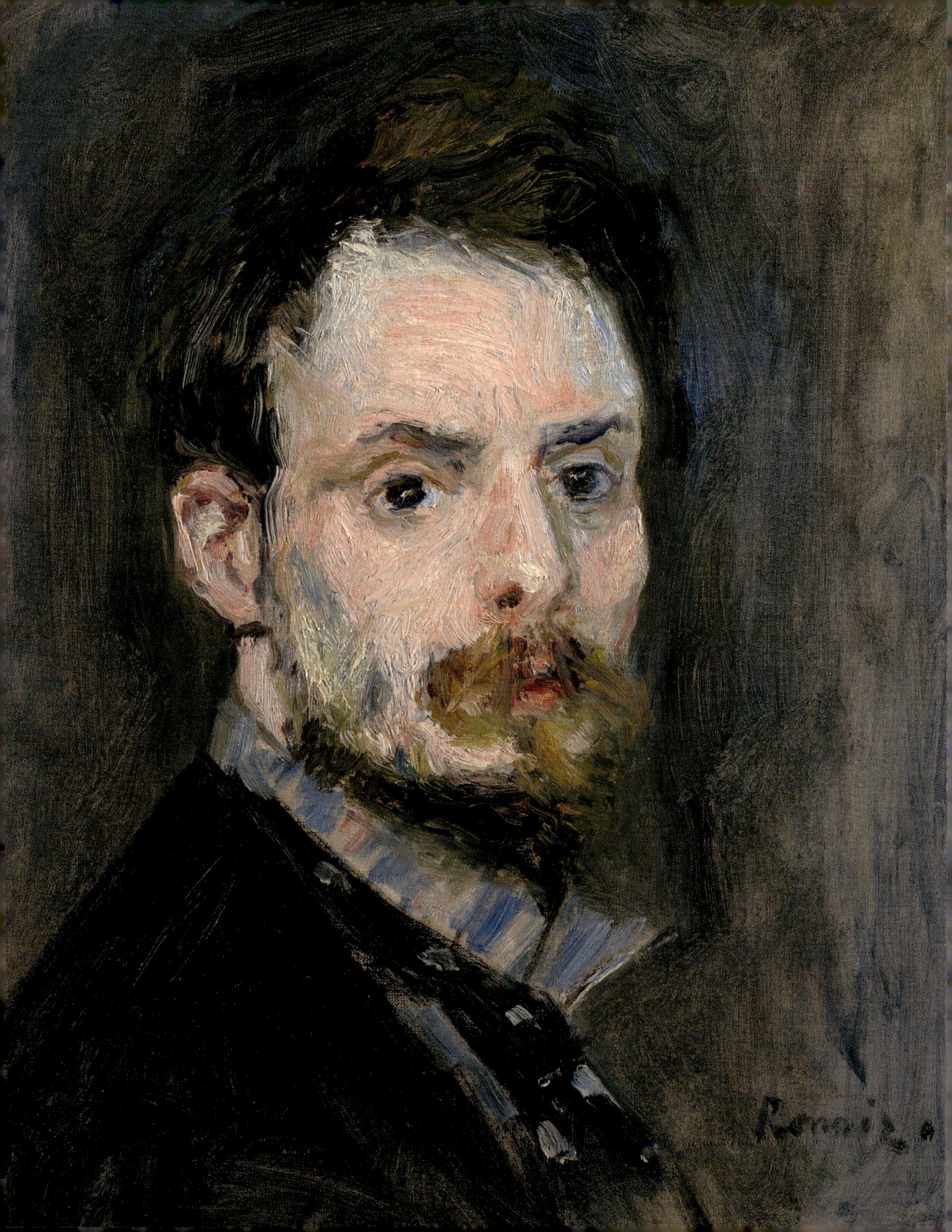
Renoir.

MASTERS OF ART

RENOIR

Alexander Adams

PRESTEL
Munich · London · New York

Front Cover: Pierre-Auguste Renoir, *Dance at Bougival*, 1883,
Museum of Fine Arts, Boston (detail, see page 87)
Frontispiece: *Self-portrait*, c. 1875, Sterling and Francine Clark Art Institute,
Williamstown, Massachusetts. Acquired by Sterling and Francine Clark before 1955
pages 8/9: Luncheon of the Boating Party, 1880/1 (see page 73)
pages 34/35: La Grenouillère, 1869 (see page 51)
pages 36/37: The Piazza San Marco, Venice, 1881 (see page 81)
pages 108/9: Pont Neuf, Paris, 1872 (see page 55)

A member of Penguin Random House Verlagsgruppe GmbH
Neumarkter Strasse 28 · 81673 Munich

1st edition 2026

produktsicherheit@penguinrandomhouse.de

A CIP catalogue record for this book is available from the British Library.

Editorial direction: Anja Besserer
Picture editing: Fiona Krech
Copyediting and proofreading: Vanessa Magson-Mann, So to Speak, Icking
Production management: Cilly Klotz
Design: Florian Frohnholzer, Sofarobotnik
Typesetting: Fotosatz Amann GmbH & Co. KG, Memmingen
Separations: Reproline mediateam
Printing and binding: Livonia Print, Riga
Typeface: Cera Pro
Paper: 150 g/m² Magno Matt
Printed in Latvia
ISBN 978-3-7913-9482-4
www.prestel.com

CONTENTS

INTRODUCTION

When we think of paintings of pleasure—those that depict, derive from and instil pleasure—we think of Pierre-Auguste Renoir (1841–1919). Renoir is rightly credited as one of the founders of Impressionism, pushing the boundaries of what could be achieved in paint and capturing optical effects of light and colour. Yet he was also the man who said, "I never thought of myself being a revolutionary painter; I just wanted to continue in the tradition of the Louvre". This book looks at how we might reconcile Renoir, the master of iconoclastic Impressionism and Renoir, the acolyte of the Louvre.

Renoir's art is synonymous with delight in the glories of life: warm weather, dappled shade, sumptuous colour, beautiful figures, moments of repose, the tender bonds of family. Not for nothing was Renoir called by 1877 a "romantic Impressionist".

Due to its explicitly pleasure-seeking and pleasure-giving nature, Renoir's art has had detractors since its public debut in the late 1860s. It has been decried as escapist and sentimental, lacking the cutting social commentary that some seek. However, once one understands Renoir better one sees not obliviousness directing his choices but a decision to spread pleasure. This explains why he would later consciously distance himself from the tenets of Impressionism without repudiating lessons he learned or the friendships he formed with fellow Impressionists.

Impressionism offered a chance to see new subjects in art and depict afresh familiar scenes and places. As critic Edmond Duranty noted in 1877, "we suffocate under the weight of the creations of past centuries", so was it any wonder the public reacted strongly to the Impressionists? Duranty concluded, "In the field of colour they made a genuine discovery for which no precedent can be found, not in the Dutch master, not the clear, pale tones of fresco painting, nor in the soft tonalities of the eighteenth century".

Renoir's working-class origins—and experience of poverty into middle age—informed his embrace of the life-improving quality of art. It played an important role in his approach to making and displaying art, which will become clear in this book. He was intensely conscious of how his art—and by extension he himself—could be rejected because of his social status. His struggle to survive as an artist, make a mark and provide for his family, did not render Renoir cynical or mercenary—although he had to be wily.

Through striving, Renoir overcame the snobbery of the art world and depicted simple pleasures, reaching into prehistory to inspire evocations of eternal delights. In making an image of a carefree paradise, Renoir inhabited a world that he thought should be available to all who wished to look at his art. In his last years, crippled and in constant pain, it was art that was his pain-killing narcotic.

Renoir once wrote to a friend regarding a journalist. "I'd be very happy if he didn't say a word about me; he can say as much as he wants about my canvases .... Painters are very boring with their pitiful stories, and people don't give a damn about them." Due to Renoir's habitual secrecy about his private life, significant biographical details relating to his family life are only now coming to light.

The recovery of letters and diaries from the artist's lifetime (efforts led by biographer Barbara Ehrlich White) continues, with newly revealed details illuminating how Renoir's situation and relationships affected his art.

Renoir's output of about 4,000 oil paintings can be (inexactly) divided into these periods: up to 1867 an academic/Realist period, 1867–1881 his Impressionist period, 1881–8 his Ingresque/Classical period, 1889–97 the Pearly (Nacreous) period, and finally 1897–1919 the Rose period. In these phases we can detect definite changes in style and palette, but also in the artist's topics. For example, city views and scenes of social leisure are typical of his Impressionist work but absent from the Rose period, which features nudes and landscapes lacking specificity in time or geography. The aim of this book is to cover the development of Renoir's art and explain how seemingly contradictory tendencies primarily stem from Renoir's taste and temperament, notwithstanding influences to which he was exposed. Perhaps most importantly, in an age that equates solemnity and sombreness with seriousness, it is worth being reminded that Renoir's art of pleasure touches the core of what it means to be human.

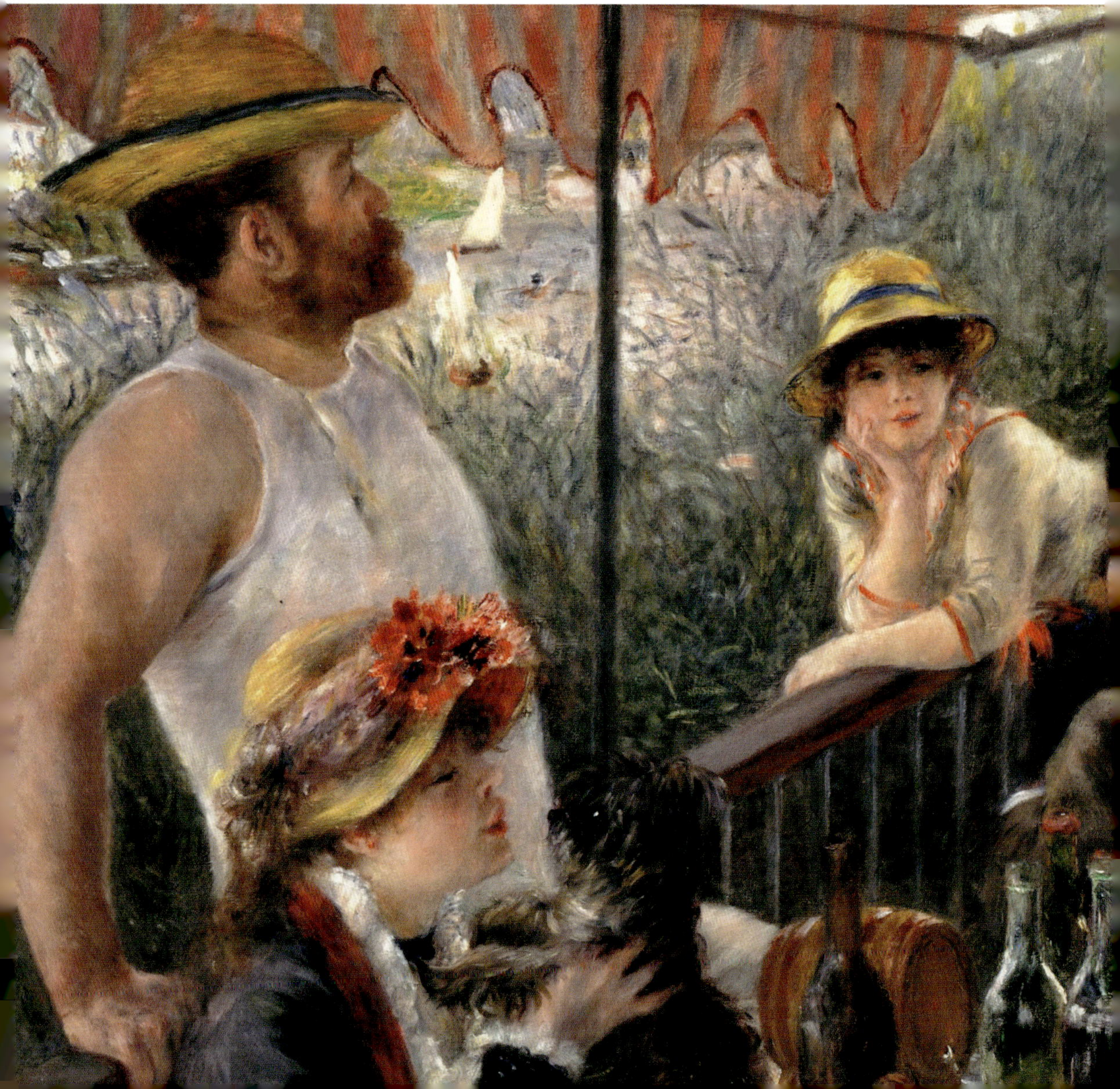

LIFE

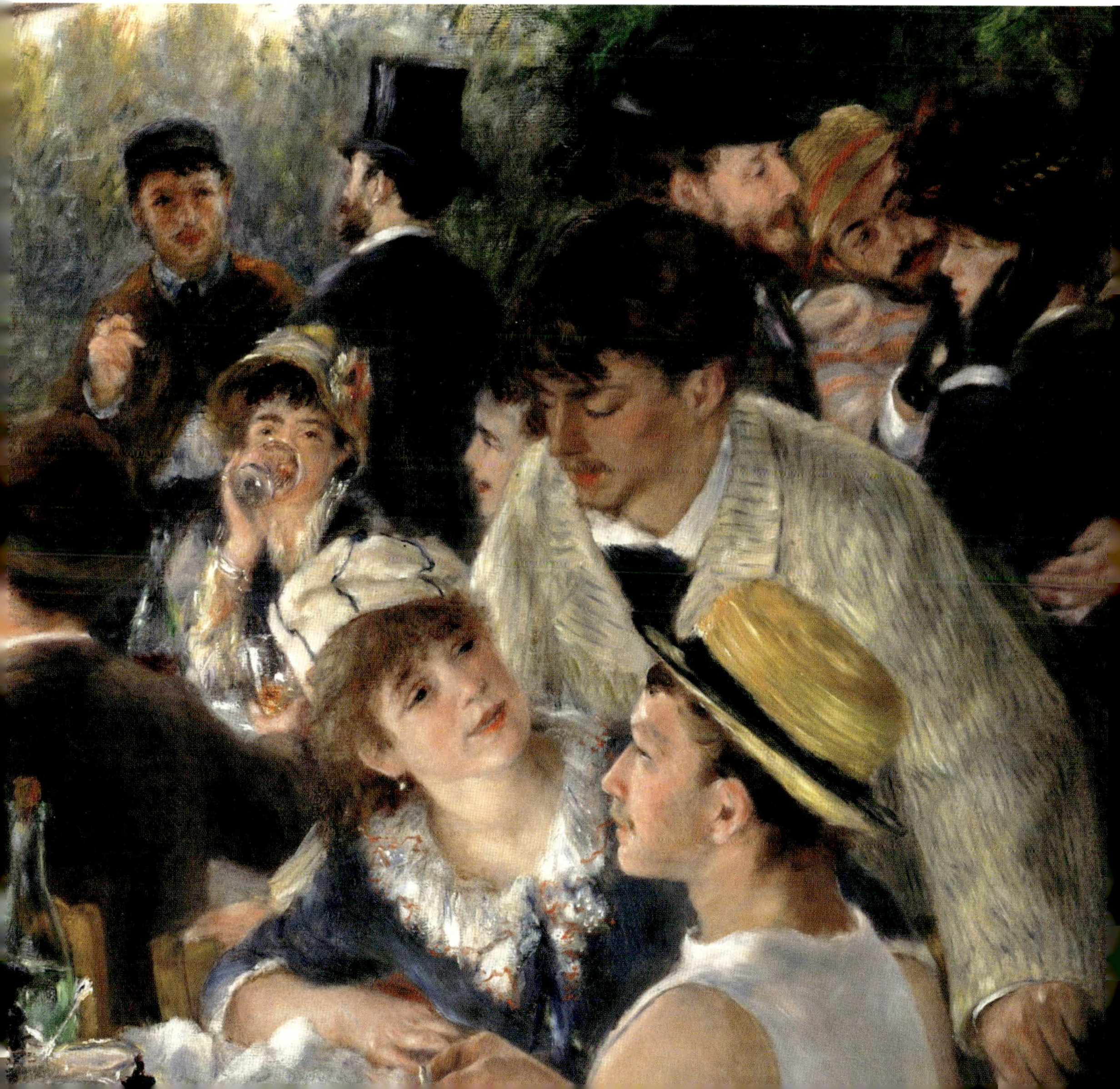

Pierre-Auguste Renoir was born in Limoges, central France, on 25 February 1841. His parents were tailor Léonard Renoir (1799–1874) and Marguerite Renoir née Merlet (1807–1896), a dressmaker. In May 1845—following the death of François, Léonard's father—the Renoir family moved to Paris. Of his siblings, it was Renoir's brother Edmond who would contribute to the future painter's success.

With this relocation, M. Renoir was attempting to better the prospects of his young and growing family of five children. The Renoirs' migration was typical of the influx of provincial poor seeking betterment. In the space of five years—which coincided with the arrival of the Renoirs—the population of Paris increased from 935,000 to 1,053,000. Baron Haussmann's modernisation campaign (page 54) led to the demolition of the Renoirs' house, located near the Louvre. This was only the most obvious manifestation of the city's growth and urbanisation in the midst of an industrial boom.

Due to poverty, the future artist—always called "Auguste"—received a limited general education. As Auguste had a talent for art, in 1854, at the age of 13, he was sent to apprentice at Lévy-Frères porcelain factory The firm produced imitations and pastiches of Rococo decorative plates, vases and lamps, which were hand painted. Designs were based on motifs originating in the art of Watteau, Lancret, Boucher and Fragonard. The process demanded a steady hand, attention to detail, consistency and accuracy, but left painters very limited scope for expression. Renoir retained a few examples of his decorated porcelain, passing them down to his family.

The painter went beyond competence and strove for excellence, studying art in greater depth than required. After factory shifts, Renoir took evening classes in drawing at a municipal art school. He frequented the Louvre, making drawings and cultivating a lasting appreciation of Giorgione, Veronese, Rubens and Delacroix, in addition to the Rococo masters. His attitudes and self-image as an artist were formed at this early age. Later, he would admit, "I am of the eighteenth century. I humbly consider not only that my art descends from Watteau, Fragonard, Hubert Robert, but even that I am one of them".

In 1858, Renoir lost his job when his role was overtaken by increasing mechanisation. The application of printed colour decals was faster and cheaper than employing artists to hand paint designs. Encroachment of mechanisation upon the livelihoods of skilled artisans contributed to Renoir's lifelong empathy with craftspeople and gave rise to an ingrained mistrust of technology and mass production. Decided upon the life of an artist, Renoir painted fans, screens and imitation stained glass for export to save money in order to support advanced study. Although Renoir tired of copying others' inventions, he never disdained decoration, voluntarily producing ceramics, bronzes and decorative paintings even after attaining artistic independence. In old age, he recalled with pleasure painting murals in twenty cafés, none of which today survive.

At this time, trainee artists studied in ateliers of master artists who prepared them for entry into the academy, the École des Beaux-Arts. Renoir studied under a drawing master called Louis Denis Caillouette, himself a sculptor. In November 1861, the artist entered the studio of Swiss painter Charles Gleyre (1806–1874), inheritor of Paul Delaroche's studio and a devotee of Ingres. The master would provide models, instruct pupils in technique and materials and provide guidance, all for the cost of 10 francs per month. This period would prove formative for Renoir not just for the technical instruction but also for the friendships he would forge. In Gleyre's studio Renoir worked alongside Claude Monet (1840–1925), Frédéric Bazille (1841–1870) and Alfred Sisley (1839–1899). Soon they would meet Paul Cézanne (1839–1906) and Camille Pissarro (1830–1903) and (in 1865) Edgar Degas (1843–1918). These painters would form the core of the movement later called Impressionism. However, at this stage these young artists were broadly united in their veneration for Gustave Courbet—a newly risen advocate of Realism, who had outraged and perturbed critics, artists and the public—and Jean-François Millet's scenes of peasant life, which had politically disruptive social connotations. (Renoir personally repudiated Millet's peasant scenes, although admiring the artist in general.) Degas would always describe himself as a Realist, never an Impressionist.

Gleyre's students—invigorated by the new landscapists Courbet, Millet and Corot—would take a short train ride to paint in Fontainebleau forest. Renoir later (somewhat implausibly) claimed that when impoverished he would walk the 38 miles there. They would paint *en plein air* (Fr: in the open air), attempting to capture exact lighting effects, considering study of nature as a proper end in itself, not—as instructed by Gleyre—just preparation for inventing scenes. Renoir said that he painted landscapes (not a subject natural for him) because he had no money for models. While painting in the forest he encountered artists he admired: Corot, Daubigny, Courbet and Narcisse-Virgile Díaz de la Peña (collectively called the Barbizon School). During one meeting Díaz told Renoir, "Never must a painter who has any respect for himself touch his brush, unless he has his model in front of him". Renoir took this advice to heart, although he was never a slave to it.

Although Renoir liked to portray himself as spurned, he did reasonably well under instruction. He was accepted through the 1 April 1862 entrance exam into the École nationale supérieure des Beaux-Arts. He would study there and in Gleyre's studio until 1864. Students attended anatomical drawing classes and theoretical classes at art school, but since it did not teach painting, students worked with independent masters for painting instruction. Throughout his studies at the École nationale Renoir did adequately in exams, although he later claimed, "The misunderstanding began as soon as I started studying at the École des Beaux-Arts. I was an extremely hard-working student; I slaved away at academic painting; I studied the classical style, but I never earned the least honourable mention, and my professors were unanimous in finding my painting execrable". Student Renoir attended dissections at the École de medicine, where he drew cadavers alongside trainee physicians. He continued to spend hours copying Old

Fréderic Bazille, *Portrait of Renoir*, 1867

Masters in the Louvre, noting much in terms of coloration, handling of paint and composition that contradicted the lessons of Gleyre and the school's professors—as did the example of the Barbizon School's anti-academic landscapes.

The year 1864 would see Renoir's departure from art school and his public debut in the autumn Salon—a jury-selected grand exhibition at the Louvre, which was the premier art event of the Parisian social calendar. A Salon appearance could make an artist's reputation and could lead to paid commissions. Unlike the rejection of the previous year, Renoir's submission in 1864 (*La Esmeralda*, based on the novel *The Hunchback of Notre Dame*) was accepted. However, it was overlooked by critics and collectors. By the time it was returned unsold to Renoir, he had decided literary subjects designed to appeal to Salon juries were inimical to his ambitions, so he destroyed the canvas. His painting *Lise, Lady with a Parasol* (1867) was a great success of the 1868 Salon, proving that it was contemporary non-narrative tableaux—not literary-historical ones—that were Renoir's forte.

At this time, Renoir and his group of friends were supporters of Édouard Manet (1832–1883), to whom the young Renoir would become close. They would attend Café Guerbois, where Manet held court from 1869 to 1875. Manet's groundbreaking *Luncheon in the Grass* (1863) had scandalised Paris, as it had implied impropriety by depicting young gentlemen in modern dress consorting with apparent prostitutes. While Courbet and Millet had exposed Parisian society to the reality of peasant life, Manet had depicted the urban middle-class at their most disreputable, which was too unpalatable for Salon-goers. In Henri Fantin-Latour's *A Studio in Batignolles* (1870)—a tribute to Manet, showing him at work and attended by admirers—the young Renoir was placed near the master. Grande rue de Batignolles was where Bazille and Renoir shared a studio. In 1869, before this group were called the "Impressionists", Renoir and his colleagues (including Fantin-Latour) were called by a critic the "School of Batignolles".

Bazille, Monet and Renoir depicted each other in the shared studios of Sisley and Bazille. They lived, worked and socialised closely, sharing ideas and models, sometimes painting outdoors together. Monet was wedded to working around Paris outdoors; Renoir would sometimes join him. The pair's paintings at Le Grenouillère in early September 1869 (page 50) are considered the first Impressionist works, stylistically speaking. Renoir depicted Monet at work outdoors in Argenteuil (pages 14/15). Monet and his wife Camille became his firm friends, with the painters supporting each other in practical and personal respects, while differing on politics. In later years, Monet would disdain official honours, even as Renoir accepted them.

During the mid-1860s, Jules Le Coeur became a close friend and confidant of the painter. Le Coeur was an upper-class Parisian who studied under Gleyre; he would later give up making paintings and instead collect them. He bought a number of Renoir paintings, including *Forest* (page 16), which depicts him walking his dogs in a place where the Batignolles Group regularly painted. Le Coeur commissioned portraits of family members from

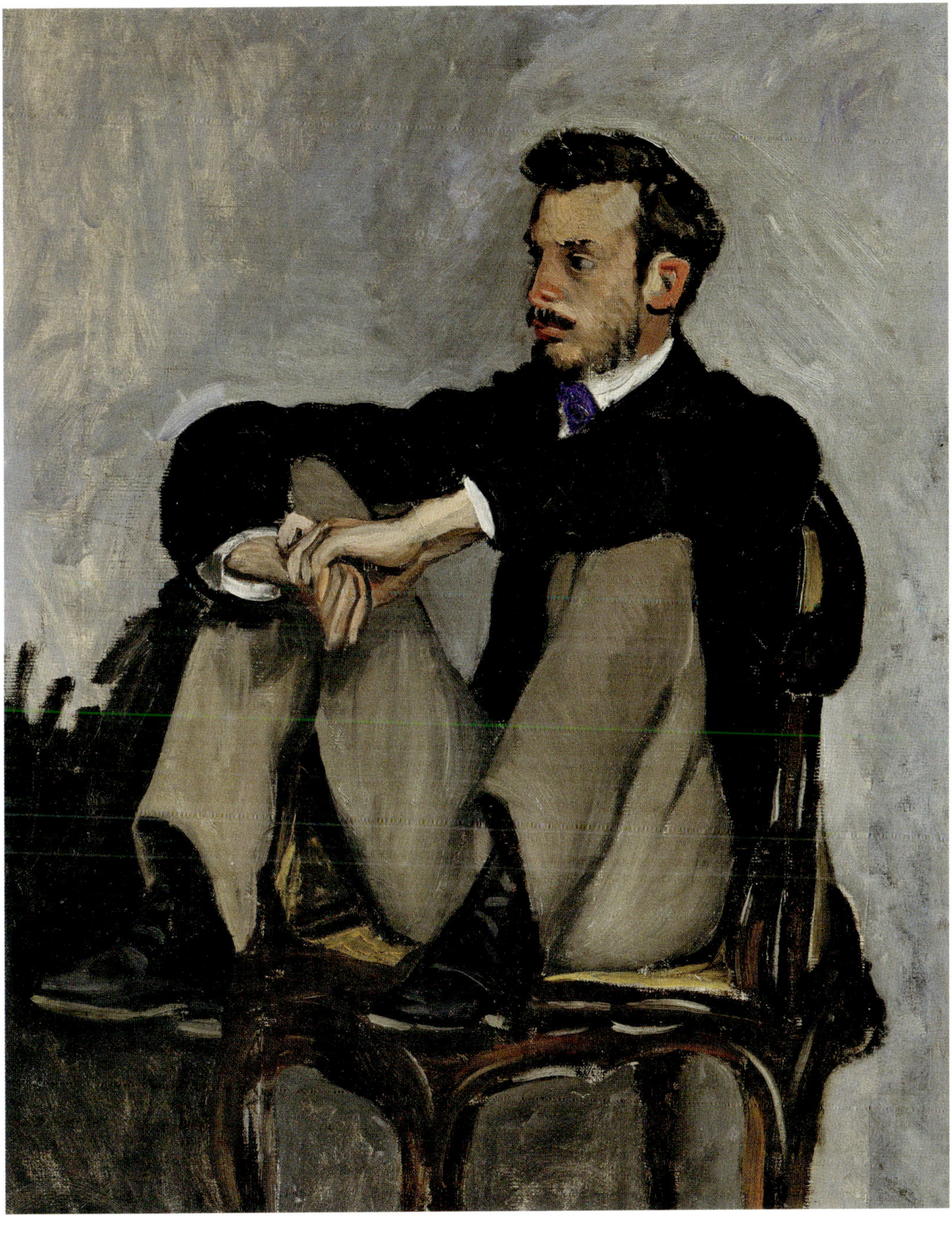

Monet Painting in his Garden at Argenteuil, c. 1873

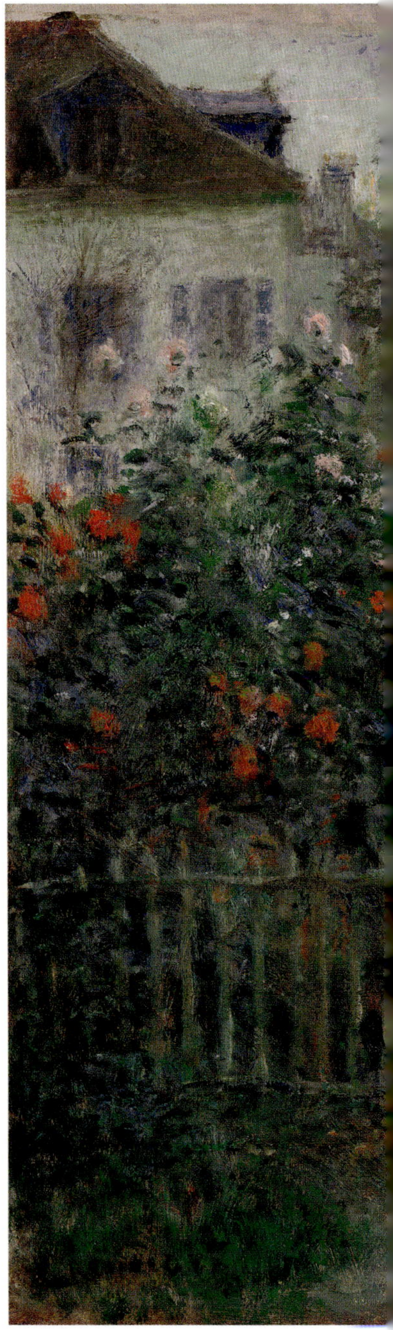

Renoir, with the latter becoming friendly with members of the Le Coeur family. The artist came to rely on portraits as a vital source of income. Between commissions, he painted artist colleagues and produced some self-portraits. When the friendship with Le Coeur ended in unclear circumstances in the summer of 1874, Renoir lost both a friend and a valued patron.

In 1866 Renoir met professional model Lise Tréhot (1848–1922). She modelled for *Diana* (page 43) and other important early pictures; she would become his lover and his only model until 1872. Lise's sister Clemence became the mistress of Jules Le Coeur. Both men would keep their affairs secret from their families. In September 1868 Lise gave birth to Renoir's son Pierre, who would apparently die in infancy—records are scant. In July 1870 Lise gave birth to a daughter Jeanne. As was common for illegitimate children, Jeanne would be given up for adoption. However, Renoir took an interest in the child's welfare and would keep in contact and provide what financial support he could, always covertly. It seems Lise was waiting for Renoir to marry her and provide her with security and status once he attained some success. However, she could not wait forever and would marry an architect in 1872, ending contact with Renoir.

The plans and routines of many were disrupted by the outbreak of hostilities following declaration of war between France and Prussia on 19 July 1870. Some colleagues, including Monet and Pissarro, would flee to London, others would be drafted. Alongside Bazille, Degas and others, Renoir was called up for military service. Renoir would serve

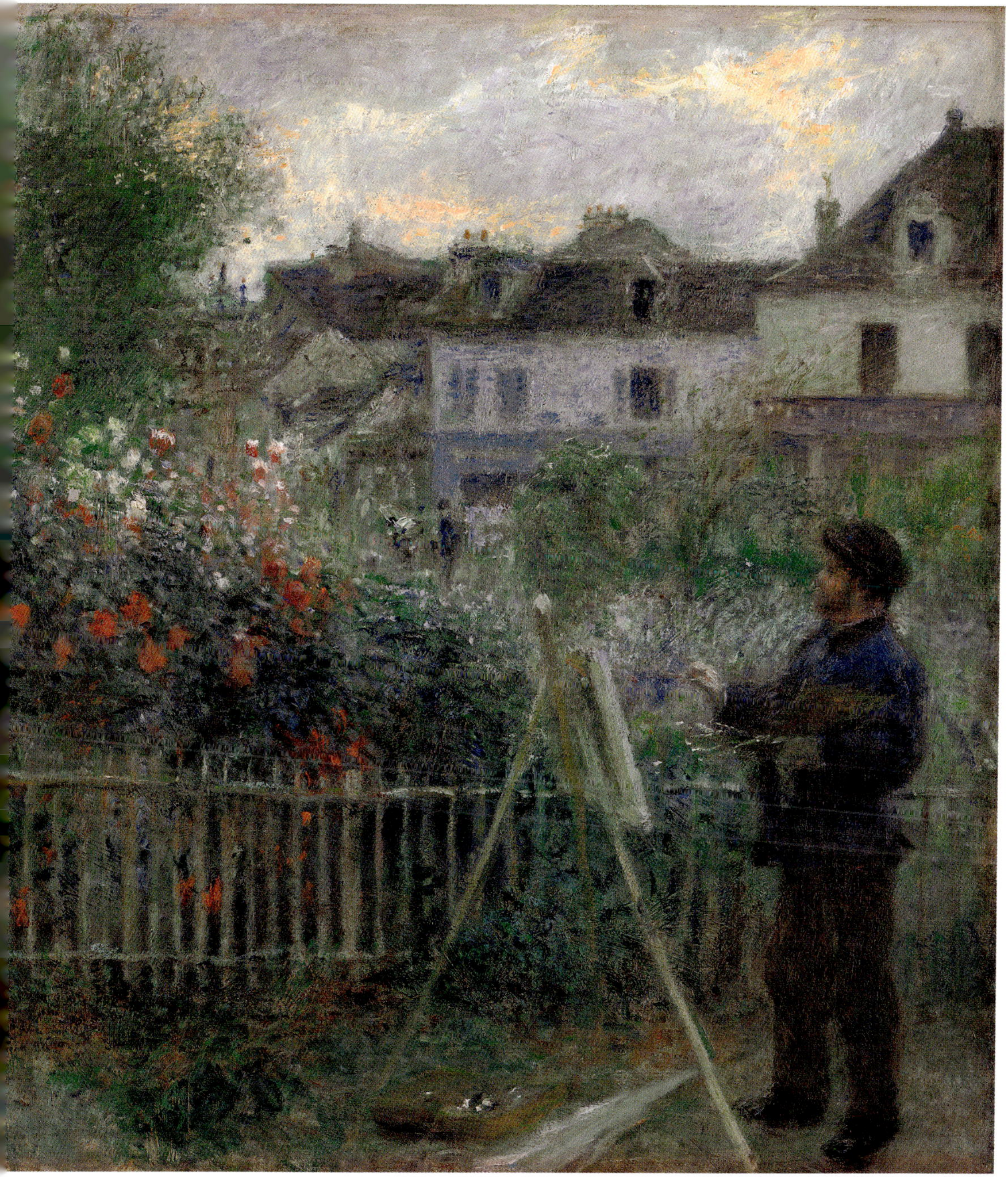

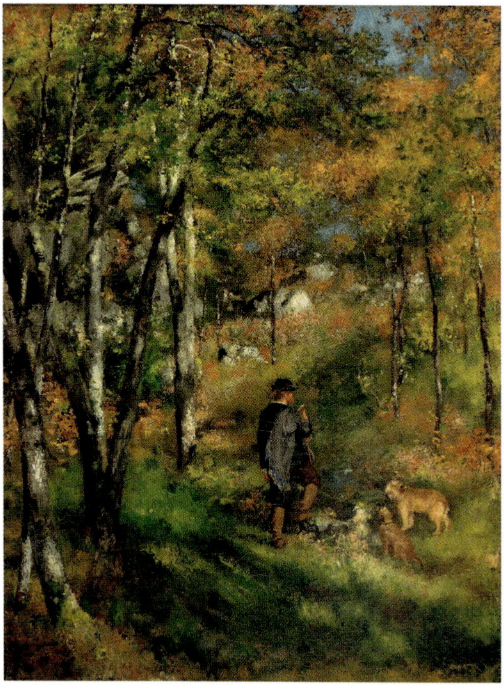

***Jules le Coeur and his Dogs, Walking in the Forest of Fontainebleau*, 1866**

with the 10th Régiment Chasseurs à Cheval (Light Cavalry), 4th Platoon, stationed far from Paris. He contracted dysentery and was too ill to see active service. Renoir would be demobilised in the spring of 1871, returning without experience of combat.

By the time Renoir was back in Paris—at the end of hostilities in mid-1871—France had lost the war, and the band of artist-brothers had lost Bazille, killed in combat on 28 November 1870. Following French defeat, the fall of Napoléon III and the occupation of Paris, a popular revolt took place. The Paris Commune of 1871 pitted dedicated republicans and socialists against the new government of France. The declaration of an independent district in Paris led to a short-lived but bloody siege. Renoir evaded military service in the revolutionary cause, towards which he was sceptical, by escaping to the nearby village of Louveciennes, where he stayed until the fall of the Commune.

Years following the turbulent events of 1870–2 would be productive for Renoir. He eschewed the most direct naturalistic depictions of light and colour and would take up subjects that reflected his social circle, working with a new technique that deployed vivid colour applied more smoothly. Women and children would feature in Renoir's pictures. He produced street views and investigated the potential of social settings—such as the opera, dance halls, cabarets and restaurants—for scenes of urban leisure. Dissimilar to the social realism of his former idols Millet and Courbet, Renoir would paint contemporary *fêtes galantes*, where real people abandoned everyday cares to flirt.

Following rejection by the Salon jury of 1872, Renoir took on the challenge of an equestrian portrait as a showpiece. The subject of *A Morning Ride in the Bois de Bologne* (1873) was Madame Henriette Darras, an acquaintance of his patron friend Le Coeur. No doubt hoping the large painting would cause a splash—and that the well-connected Le Coeur could lure collector friends—Renoir was disappointed by this fresh rejection. In fairness, *A Morning Ride* is not a successful painting; the horses appear stiff and unconvincing, making the work an awkward montage.

This canvas was subsequently exhibited in the Salon des Refusés of May 1873. The show was comprised of works rejected by the Salon jury, serving as an alternative to the official exhibition. Members of the School of Batignolles were frustrated that

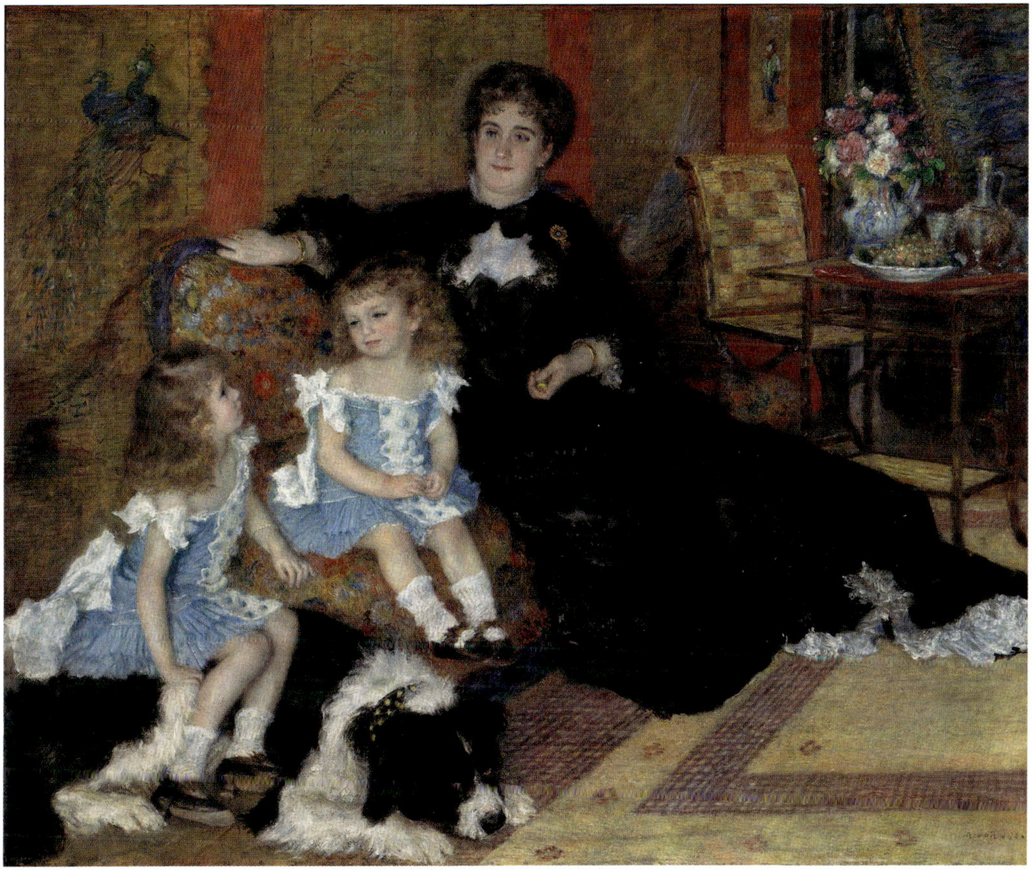

Madame Charpentier and her Children, 1879

pandering to the expectations of Salon juries was distorting their production. Renoir, Monet, Degas, Pissarro, Sisley, Cézanne, Armand Guillaumin, Berthe Morisot (page 96) and others needed to curate their own exhibitions in order to have the freedom they craved. On 27 December 1873, Renoir was one of the founders of the Société Anonyme des Artistes Peintres, Sculpteurs, Graveurs, which would hold its initial exhibition in April 1874—the first of eight exhibitions by the group called "The Impressionists".

One notable absence was Manet. Although invited to participate, he declined. Manet considered the Salon the most appropriate arena for advances in art. Renoir was ambivalent. He was dismissive of the conservatism of the Salon jury, but he was—still poor and unable to support his own family—anxious for access to potential patrons, who could best be reached through the Salon. Renoir decided year by year as to whether to submit to the Salon and participate in Impressionist exhibitions. As a scholar Nicole R. Myers puts it, "His production between

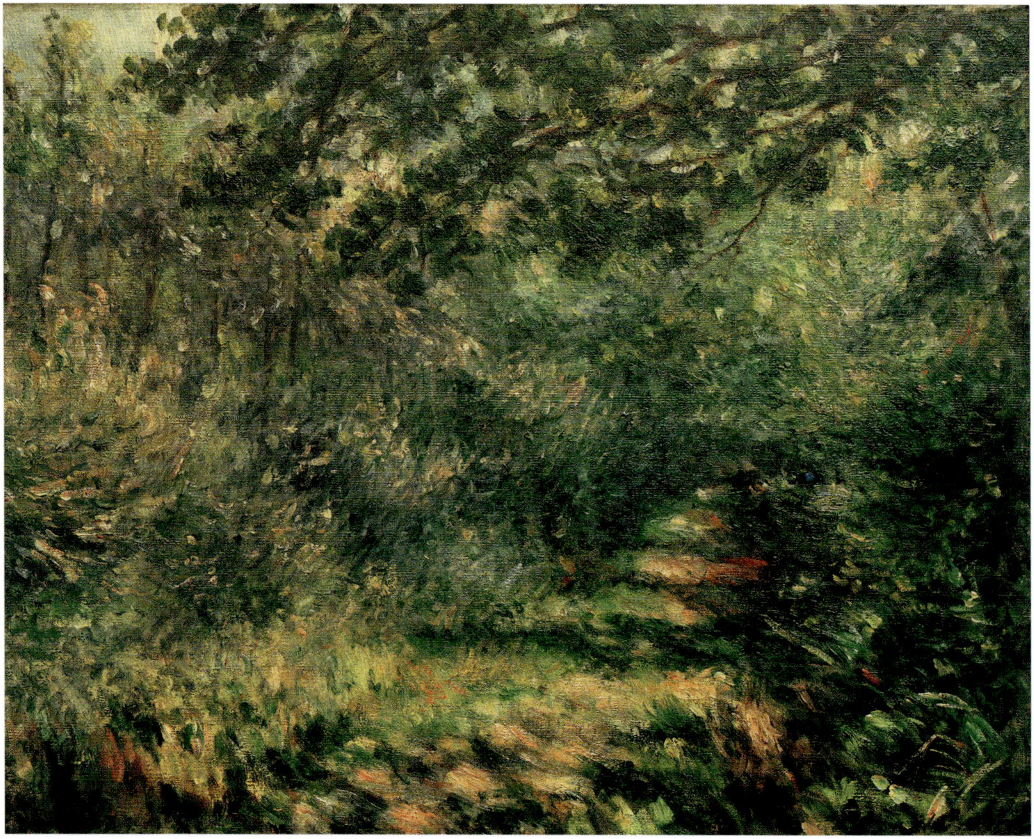

The Woodland Path, 1874–1880

1863 and 1876 can be seen as oscillating between these two distinct poles in an attempt to find a balance between the timelessness and stability of classical art and down-to-earth ephemerality of Realism". Renoir himself said, "In Paris there are scarcely fifteen art-lovers able to appreciate a painter outside the Salon .... I don't want to waste my time nursing a grievance against the Salon. I don't even want to seem to be doing so. I believe you should just paint as you can. That's all".

This flexibility and pragmatism was typical of Renoir. He was a complex man. In the studio he drenched his art in the most tender sentiments and pleasurable colours; out of the studio he was tense and nervous, fidgeting and chain-smoking. He was intensely self-critical. He gave the impression of a passive individual but when protecting his interests and supporting friends he could be tenacious. It served him to be seen as amiable, if only to conceal his adamantine will. Similarly, he would help family members and (before his marriage) his mistresses in secret, using deception to protect both them and himself from social opprobrium.

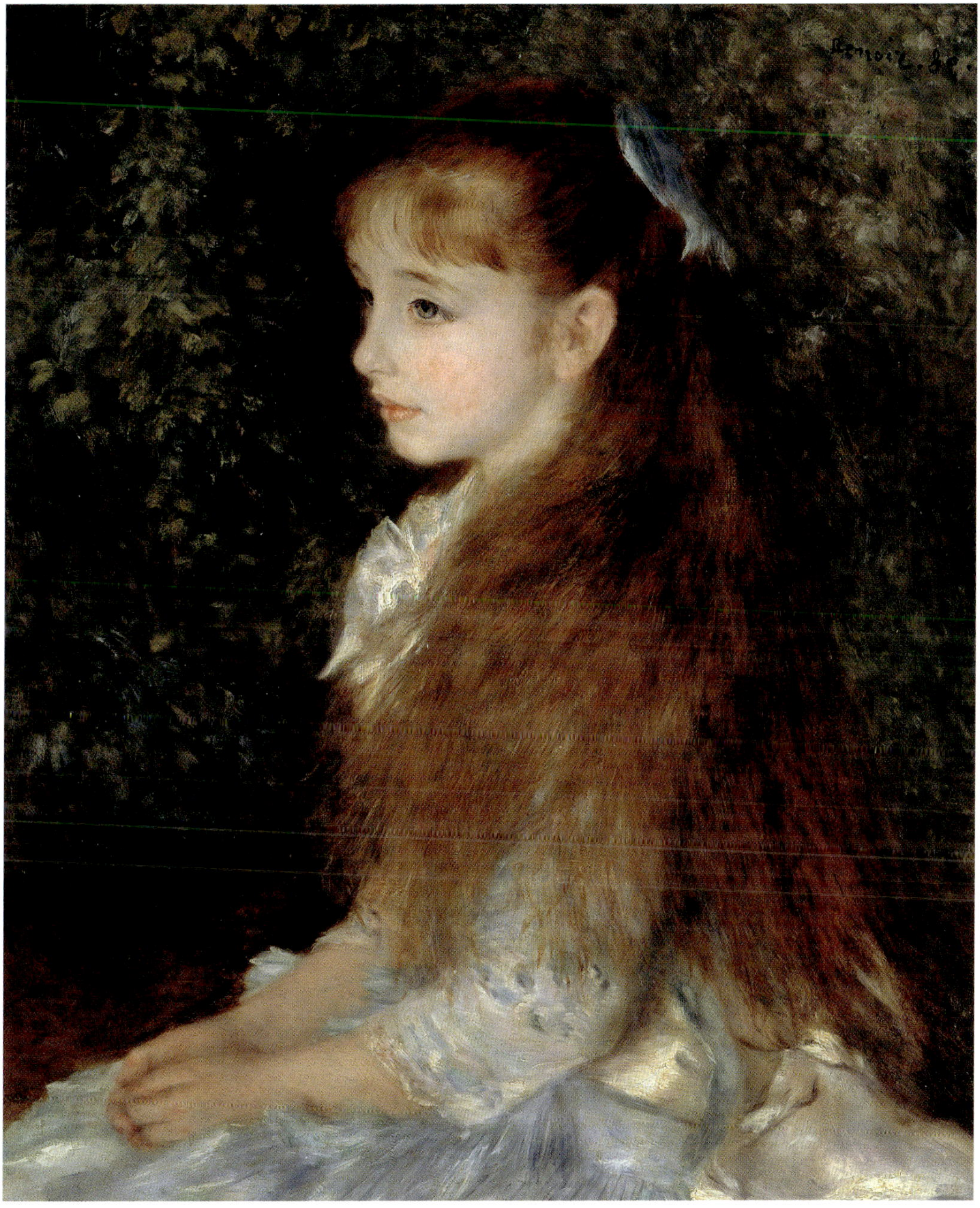

Irene Cahen d'Anvers, c. 1880

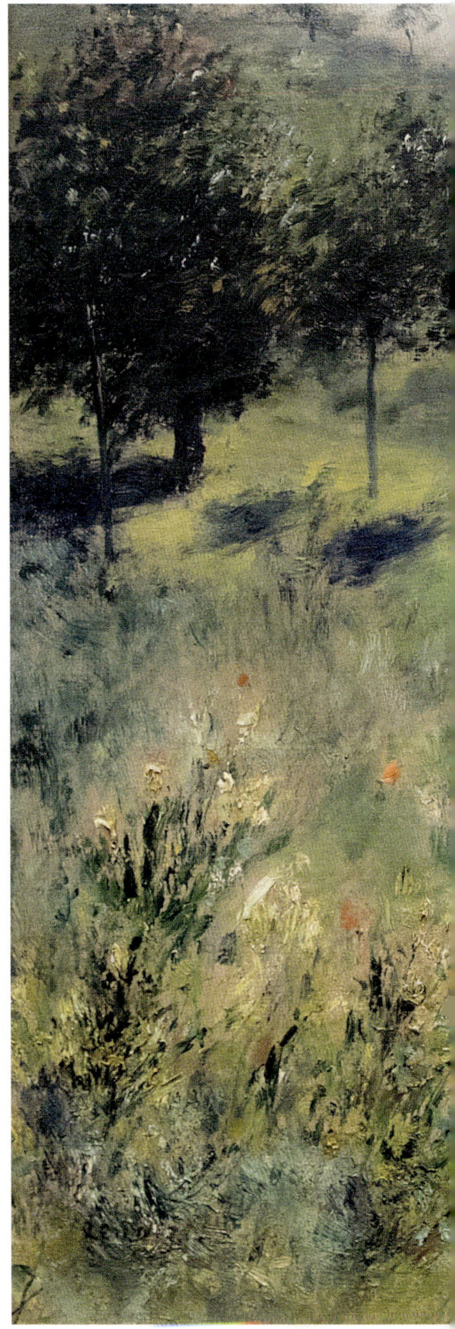

Country Footpath in Summer, 1875

Renoir's self-portrait—painted in 1875, between the first and second Independent exhibitions—reveals an artist caught between different currents (page 6). He is tense and alert, neither a dandy bohemian nor a respectable gentleman. Always pale and slim, there is a hint of poverty-induced undernourishment about Renoir's appearance. The predominant impression is of a man in a situation of struggle, both internal and external, whose apparent frailty conceals a core of indomitable strength.

Despite enthusiasm for advanced Impressionist painting technique, Renoir's taste was strongly conservative. He rejected the Symbolism of Baudelaire and the progressive social novels of Victor Hugo and Émile Zola, preferring classic literature. He was dismissive of Seurat's Pointillism and regretted that Pissarro followed Seurat. Ever complicated, Renoir was against emancipation for women—while admiring the talent of Morisot—and was suspicious of Jewish influence, despite having Jewish collectors and dealers as friends. Renoir wanted to distance himself from Pissarro, who was Jewish, because of Pissarro's vocal and persistent support for anarchism; personal association might cause people to assume Renoir was also agitating for insurrection. "To exhibit with Pissarro, Gauguin and Guillaumin would be as if I were exhibiting with some Socialist group. Before long Pissarro will be inviting [anarchist] Lavrof or some other revolutionary. The public doesn't like anything smelling of politics, and at my age I certainly don't want to become a revolutionary." He also was repelled by the shallow materialism of modern French society.

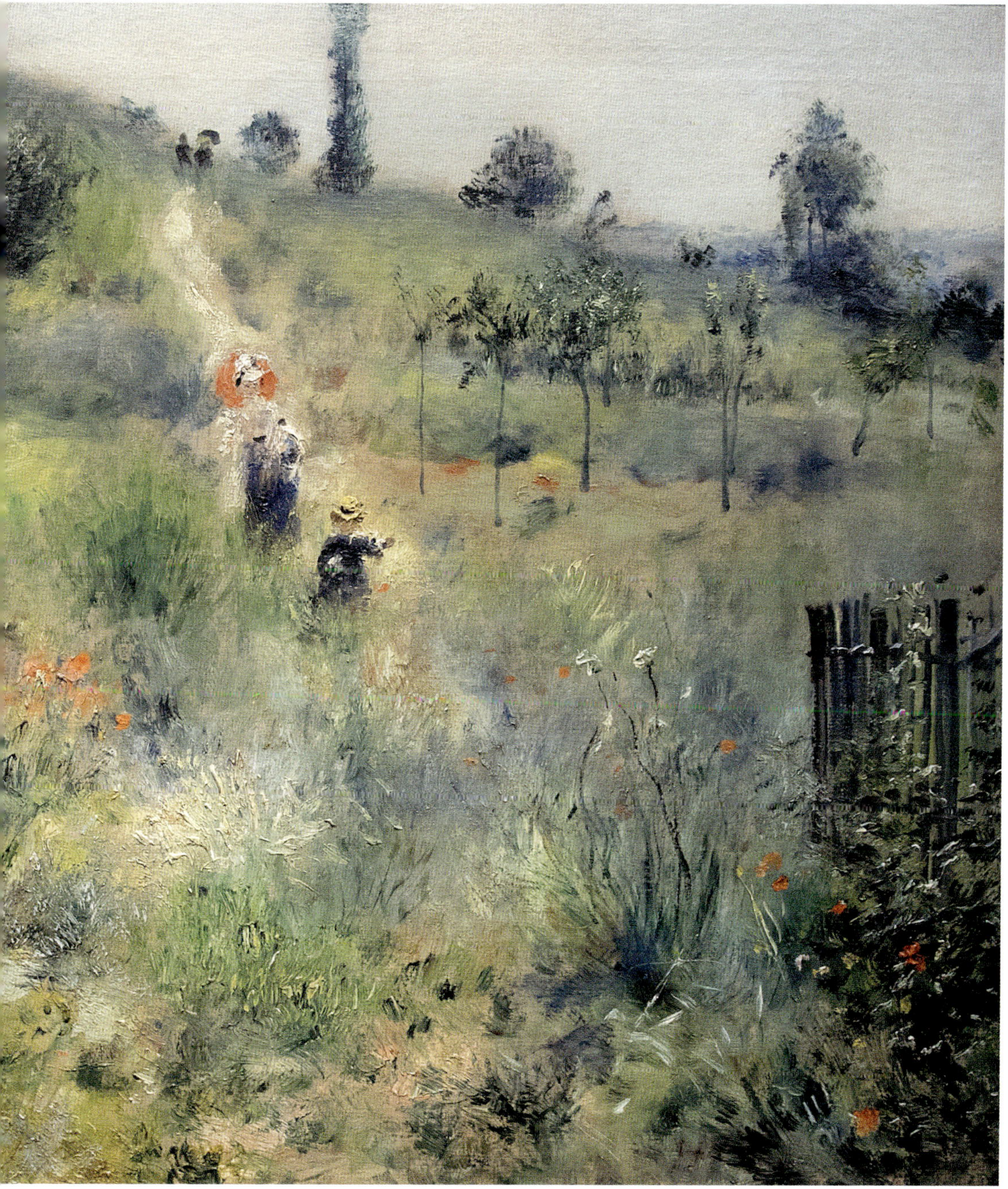

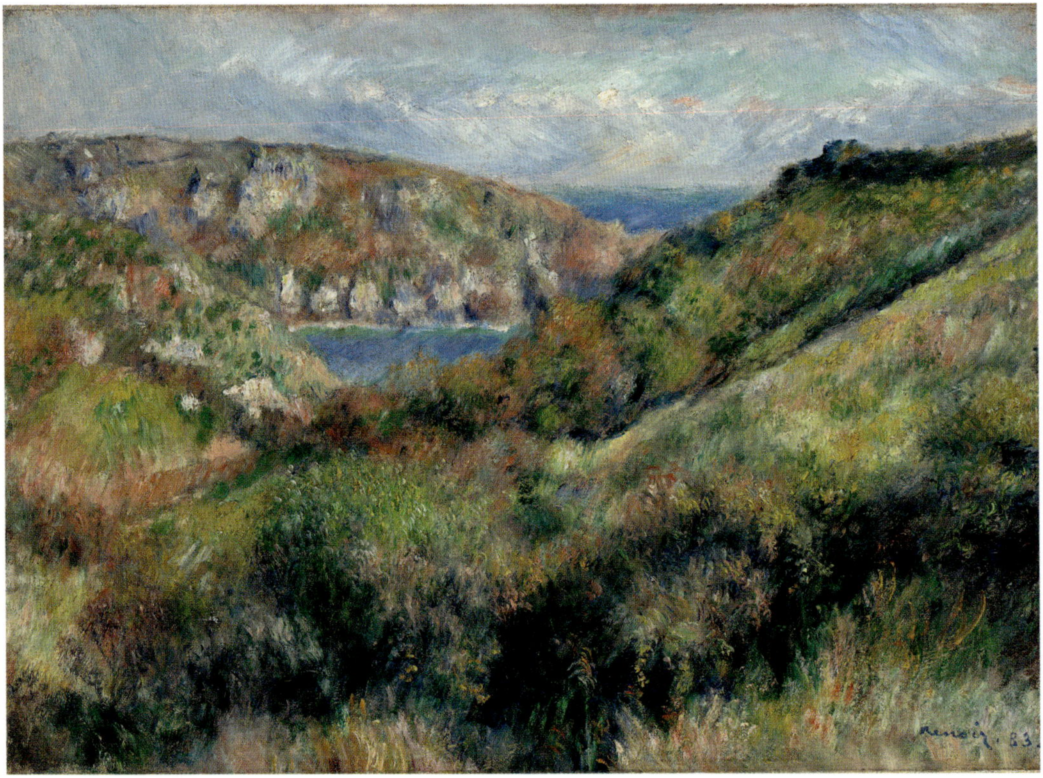

Hills around the Bay of Moulin Huet, Guernsey, 1883

The first Independent (Impressionist) exhibition got critical, mostly negative, attention but sold little, so little in fact that unsold pieces were auctioned at Hôtel Drouot on 24 March 1875 to pay the society's debts, fetching derisively low prices. A second Independent exhibition in 1876 received similar critical and commercial rejection. Nonetheless, dedicated and shrewd collectors were starting to gather around the new movement. One of these was Victor Chocquet, who commissioned family portraits from Renoir. The wealthy Protestant family named the Berards bought pictures, as did a number of Jewish collectors, such as the Cahen d'Anvers family, which commissioned a portrait of their daughter (page 19). Paul Durand-Ruel (1831–1922) would become Renoir's most important dealer by 1881, buying work directly from the painter's studio. Gradually, Renoir was lifting himself out of poverty.

François Fosca describes the painter's routine: "He was always extremely industrious, and used to start work at eight in the morning. He did not stop till midday, when he lunched at a little restaurant across the way, after which he went back to work till five o'clock. The evenings were reserved for his friends; the most constant of these were [author] Georges Rivière, the painters Franc-Lamy and Cordey, an official of the Ministère de l'Intérieur named [Eugène-Pierre] Lestringuez, and the indefatigable traveller Paul Lhôte." These men would appear in individual portraits and scenes of socialising throughout Renoir's time in Paris.

Country Footpath in Summer (1875) (page 19) is a good example of Renoir treating a subject more commonly approached by Sisley, Pissarro and Monet. Figures in meadows, gardens and by rivers were appealing to the public; it was only the loose technique and strong colours that perturbed potential buyers. In 1878 Renoir spent the summer at Pourville near Dieppe, painting sea views. He worked on small canvases that were easy to transport. In the studio he also made pastels and watercolours, but he apparently found pastel an uncongenial medium. The surviving body of about 800 drawings by Renoir is startlingly modest, considering his long and prolific career, especially compared to 3,000 surviving drawings by Pissarro. We find both drawings of motifs made for pleasure and sheets used in preparation for oil paintings. Renoir virtually never used sketchbooks.

The artist returned to exhibit at the Salon in 1878. He had achieved a degree of independence due to the support of banker Paul Berard, who commissioned a decoration for his house. Renoir would skip the 1880 and 1881 Impressionist exhibitions. The majority of his foreign travel would be undertaken over the 1881–3 period. In addition to spending time painting with Cézanne in l'Estaque, Aix, Renoir visited Algiers early in 1881 and again in mid-March to late April 1882. After initial frustration at rainy weather, Renoir would be impressed by the light and the fertility of the landscape. Finding it difficult to get models, he would concentrate on painting views. After spending the summer of 1881 in Dieppe, he would tour Italy in autumn, travelling south from Venice to Palermo in Sicily via Rome, Naples, Pompeii, Capri and Calabria.

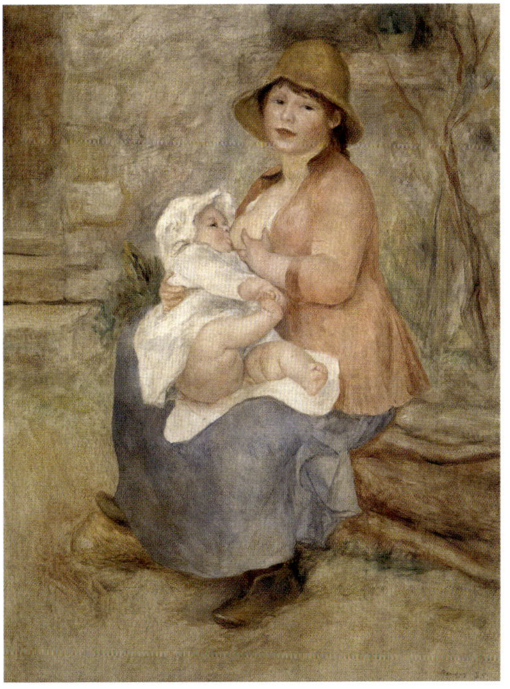

Maternity, 1885

In Palermo, the artist was granted a brief audience with Wagner and was the only person permitted to depict the composer from life. Renoir and others count the resultant painting as essentially unfinished, notable only for its subject. In Rome, Raphael's frescoes astonished the painter, which—combined with a renewed love of Ingres—would prompt a noticeable stylistic change over the winter of 1881/2. The artist would visit the Channel Islands to paint marine views, returning the following year (page 22). In 1882 an emboldened Renoir once again declined to exhibit with the

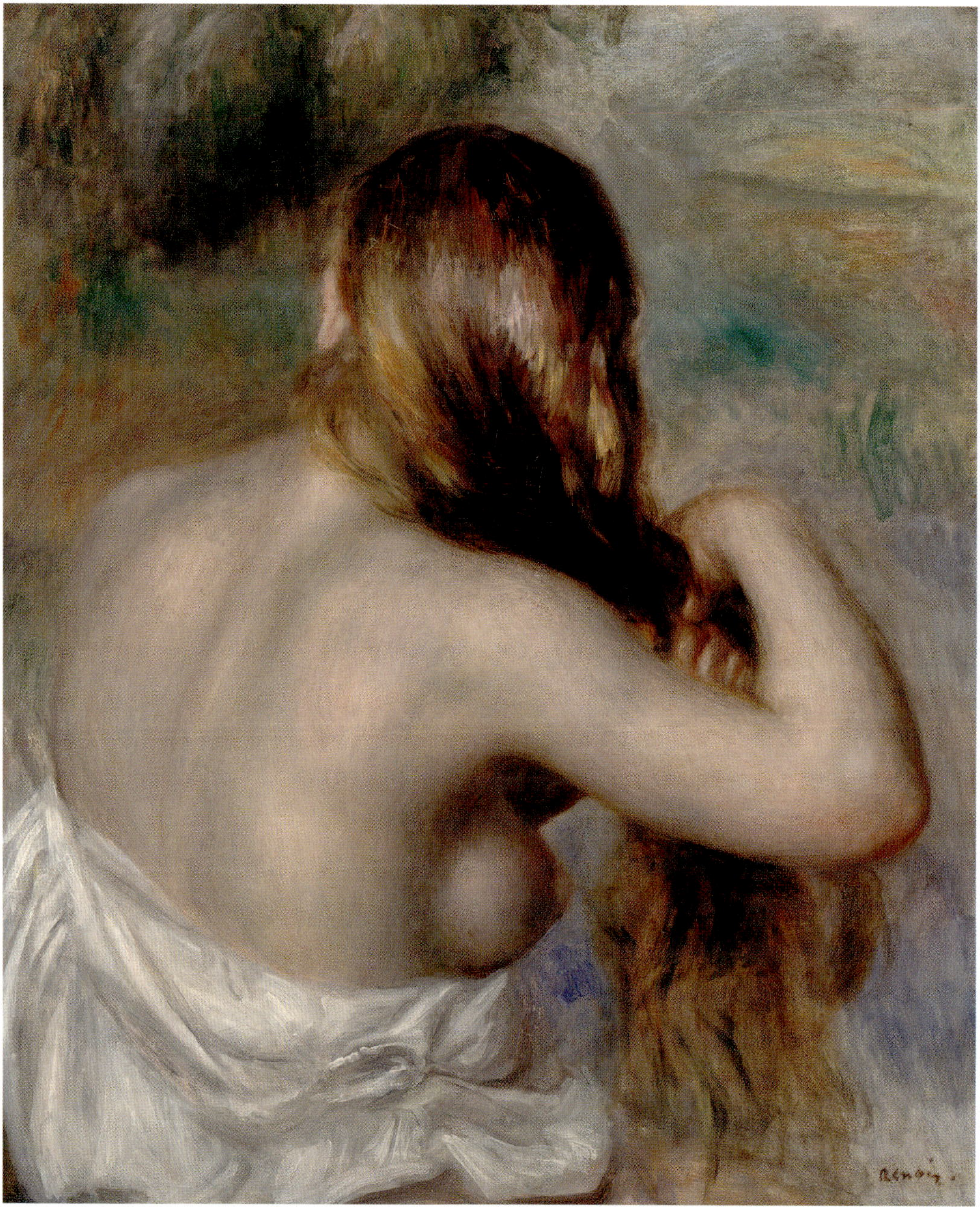

Blonde Braiding her Hair, 1886

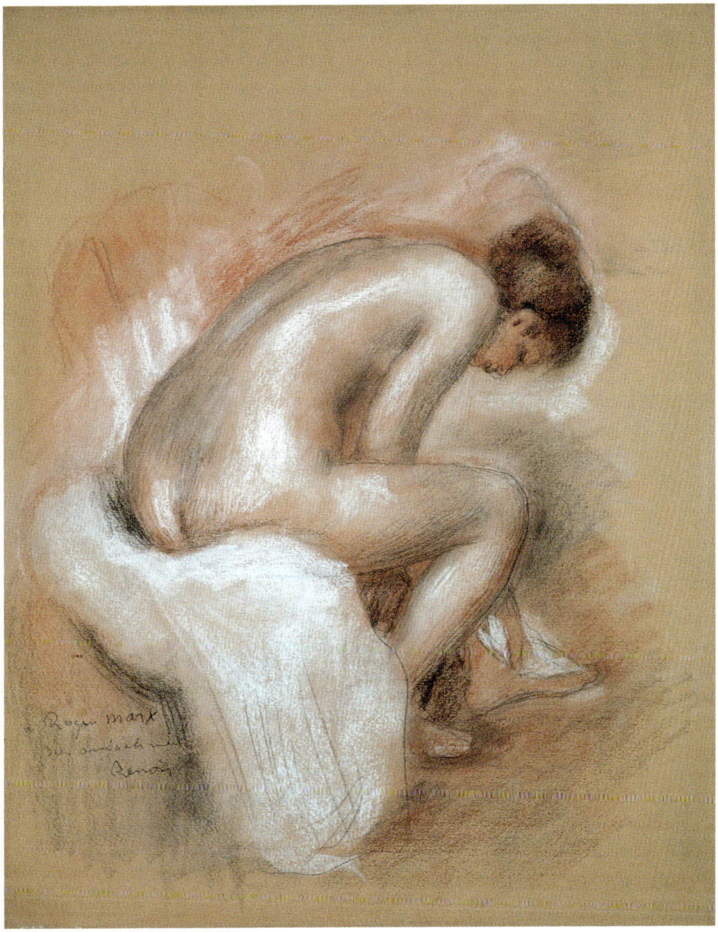

Seated Woman Bathing, 1885

Impressionists, although Durand-Ruel would loan twenty-five Renoir canvases for the exhibition from his stock.

Before returning to Renoir's life, we should examine his 1884 proposal to found a new society called "The Irregularists". "The works of nature are infinitely varied, from the greatest to the least, regardless of species", Renoir wrote. Similarly, "the churches we describe as Gothic—which are based on geometrical principles—never have a single exactly straight line". "Take a column. If I make it symmetrical with a compass, it loses its vital principle." Artists should adhere to these rules and reject "regularity, aridity and that mania for false perfection which leads us today to take the engineer's blueprint as our ideal". Although some historians consider this a satire—and Renoir certainly did have an aversion to theorisation—it does seem serious in intent. It makes sense that Renoir, concerned about appearing too much of a revolutionary, wanted to establish a conservative movement outside the Salon system that distanced him from Pissarro and Monet's progressive politics. Although the Irregularist proposal was never published or acted upon, it shows Renoir keen to forge a new path founded upon a return to ancient principles.

What Renoir did not tell anyone at the time was that when he travelled to Italy in 1881, he did not go alone. With him was Aline Charigot (1859–1915). The daughter of a family of vintners in the Aube region, Aline was an attractive woman with long blonde hair; she would become Renoir's model and mistress. She would later bear his children and they would be married. Over 1882–6 Renoir would work also with a new model, Suzanne Valadon (1865–1938). A great beauty, Valadon would become a recognisable presence in Renoir's classic paintings and later went on to become a serious painter in her own right. This coincides with Renoir adopting a new style, called his Classical or Ingresque period. We find forms more closely defined; the range and amount of broken colour is reduced; the volume of figures becomes important and shading becomes more delicate, aided by extensive glazing.

Renoir's close collaboration with Bazille, Monet and Degas never entailed giving up his critical faculties, independence and willingness to draw upon the past in order to surpass himself so as to transport viewers into the picture space. Nor did Renoir ever give up the use of glazes—suspensions of pigment in transparent varnish—which was part of the array of traditional techniques taught by Gleyre. Monet and other Impressionists came to eschew glazes, which require careful application (often applied on a horizontally positioned surface) and cannot be used over fresh paint. In contrast, Renoir never renounced glazes in favour of the *alla prima* (It: wet-on-wet) painting technique, which he also deployed on occasion. He would apply translucent glazes of purple to skies, leaving conservatives aghast.

The exhibition of *The Great Bathers* (1884–7) (page 93) marked the end of Renoir's Ingresque period. Henceforward, Renoir would adopt a blended style of the colour and energy of Impressionism along with an attention to volumetric modelling of the Ingresque period, called the Pearly or Nacreous period. Not just this change of style would make 1888 a momentous year. In 1888 Renoir suffered an attack of rheumatoid arthritis, which wracked him with pain and left him partially immobile. Although this bout was temporary, the illness would prove to be progressive. A series of hugely profitable exhibitions of Impressionism, starting in 1888 and arranged by Durand-Ruel in New York made Renoir's art increasingly valuable. His financial worries became a thing of the past and he was able to marry Aline on 14 April 1890. The arrival of three sons by Aline—Pierre (1885–1952), Jean (1894–1979) and Claude (1901–1969)—would enrich Renoir's life, now centred on his house in Essoyes (Aline's home village), situated to the south-east of Paris.

In the 1890s, the appearance of new dealers, including the Bernheim family and Ambroise Vollard

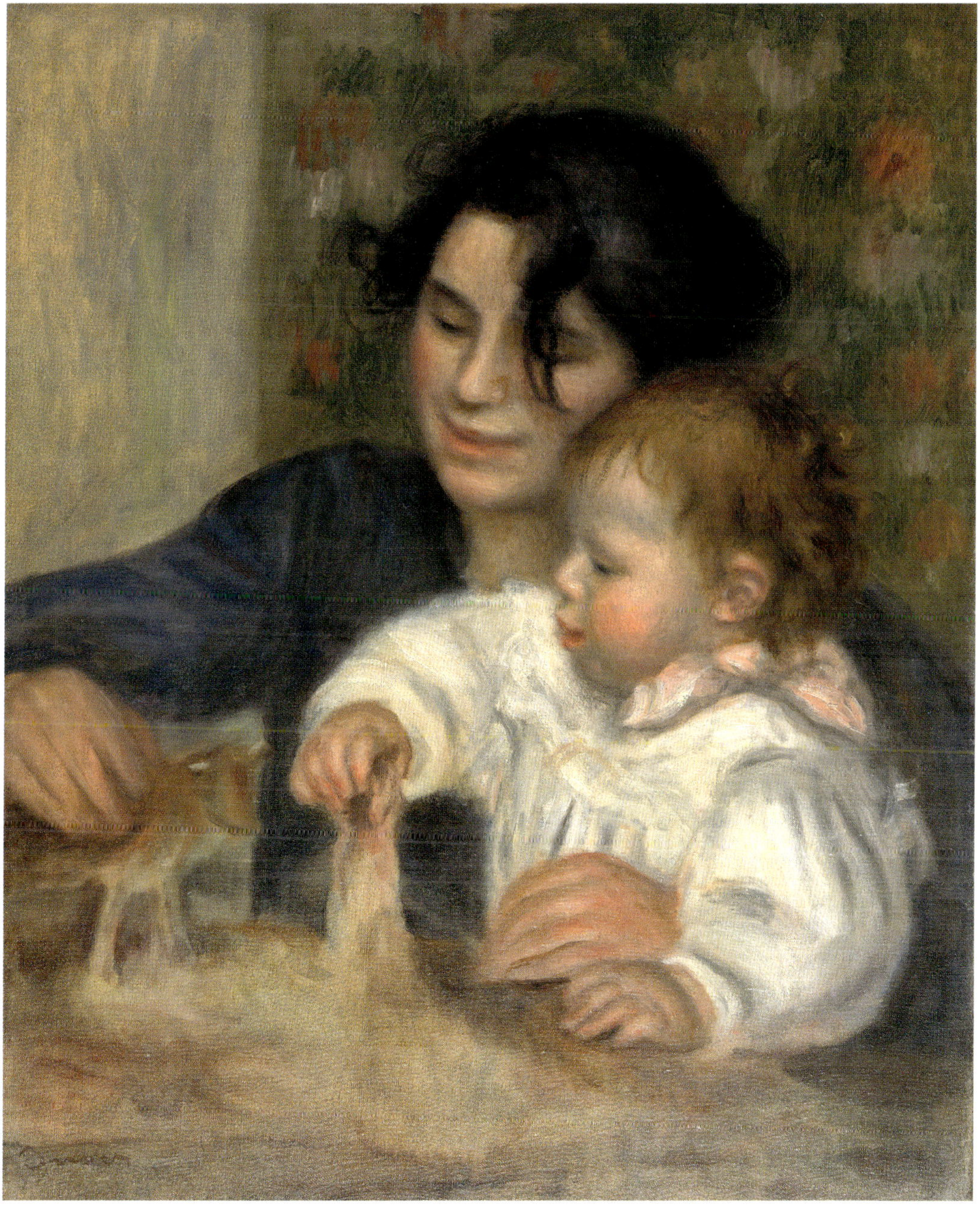

Gabrielle and Jean, 1895/6

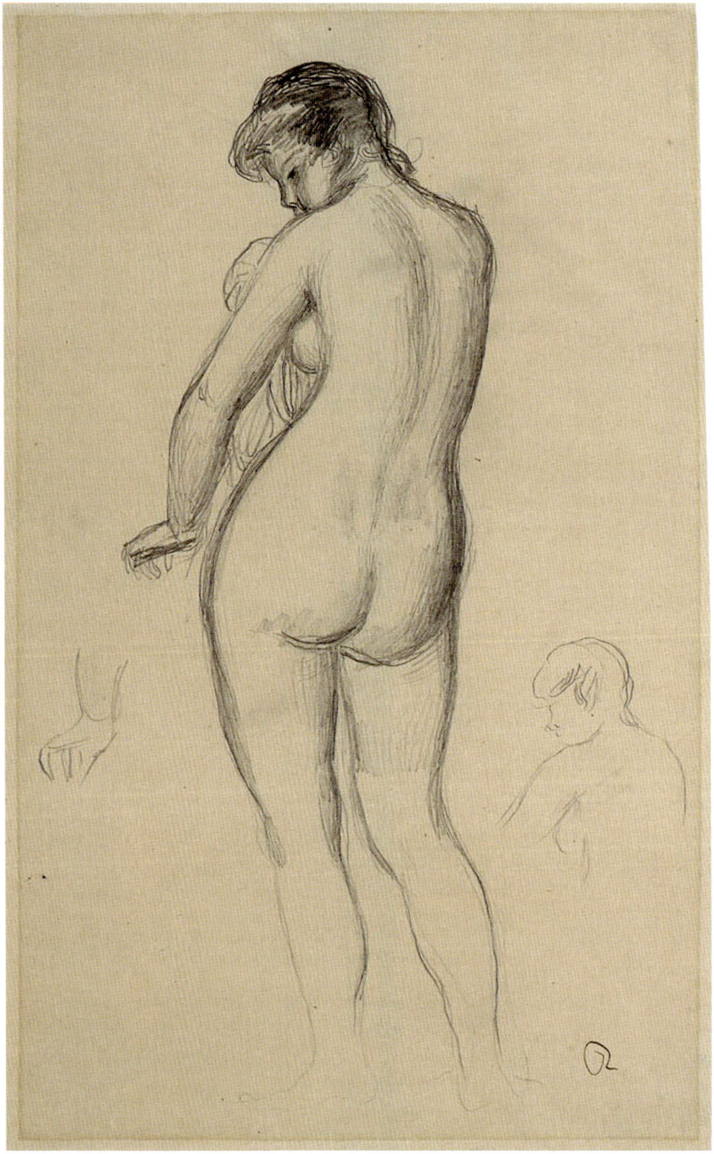

Female Nude, c. 1890/1

Caryatids, c. 1910

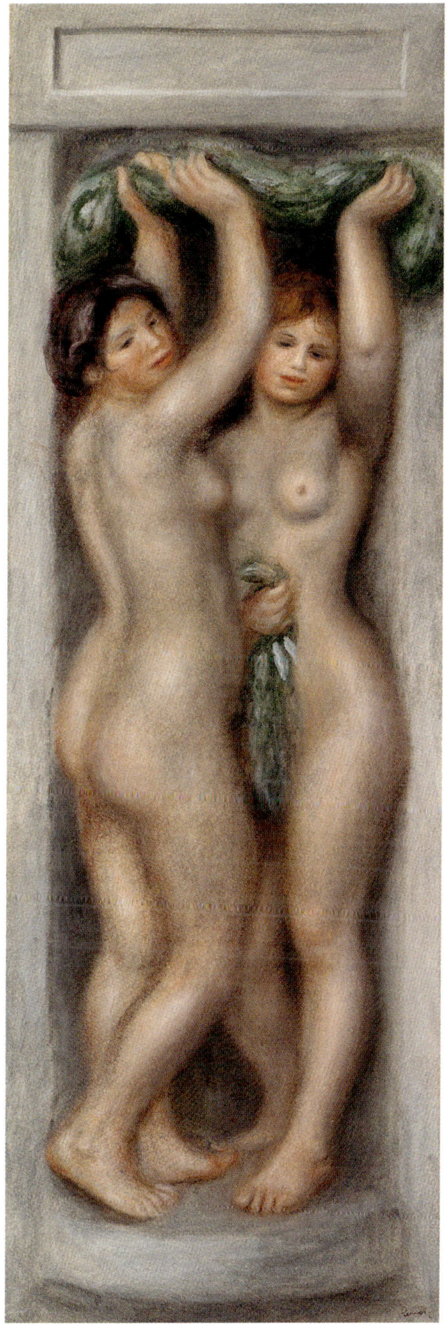

(1866–1939), would make Renoir's art more publicly accessible. Vollard made special efforts to record Renoir's ideas and life in a biography. The painter made several portraits of the vain and sensitive Vollard, including one of him as a connoisseur (page 30). He encouraged Renoir to make prints and sculpture (page 31). During this decade the artist exhibited widely, including with the Les XX and La Libre Esthétique groups in Brussels and had a solo exhibition in Paris in 1891. He travelled to Spain twice, partly to see Velázquez's art firsthand in the Prado Museum. He visited Pont Aven, Brittany, then home to Gauguin. However, Renoir felt Gauguin's art went too far in adopting foreign idioms and never concurred with Degas's esteem for the young painter.

A new presence appears in Renoir's painting at this time. Gabrielle Renard (1878–1959) was a cousin of Aline's, who joined the Renoir household in 1894. At first, she would act as a maid and nanny for Jean. Soon, she would pose for Renoir and later act as an assistant and carer for the increasingly fragile artist. The demands of motherhood and ill-health meant that Aline posed less and less during the 1890s.

Renoir's first visit to Cagnes-sur-Mer, on the Mediterranean coast of France, was in 1898. Eventually, he would spend evermore time in the Midi, where the hot weather lessened his pain and immobility. The household became more fragmented and mobile as Renoir (after years of visiting) acquired a house called Les Collettes near Cagnes in 1907. This was the first home he owned. Prosperity did not change Renoir, who had no desire to own possessions. The Mediterranean atmosphere prompted

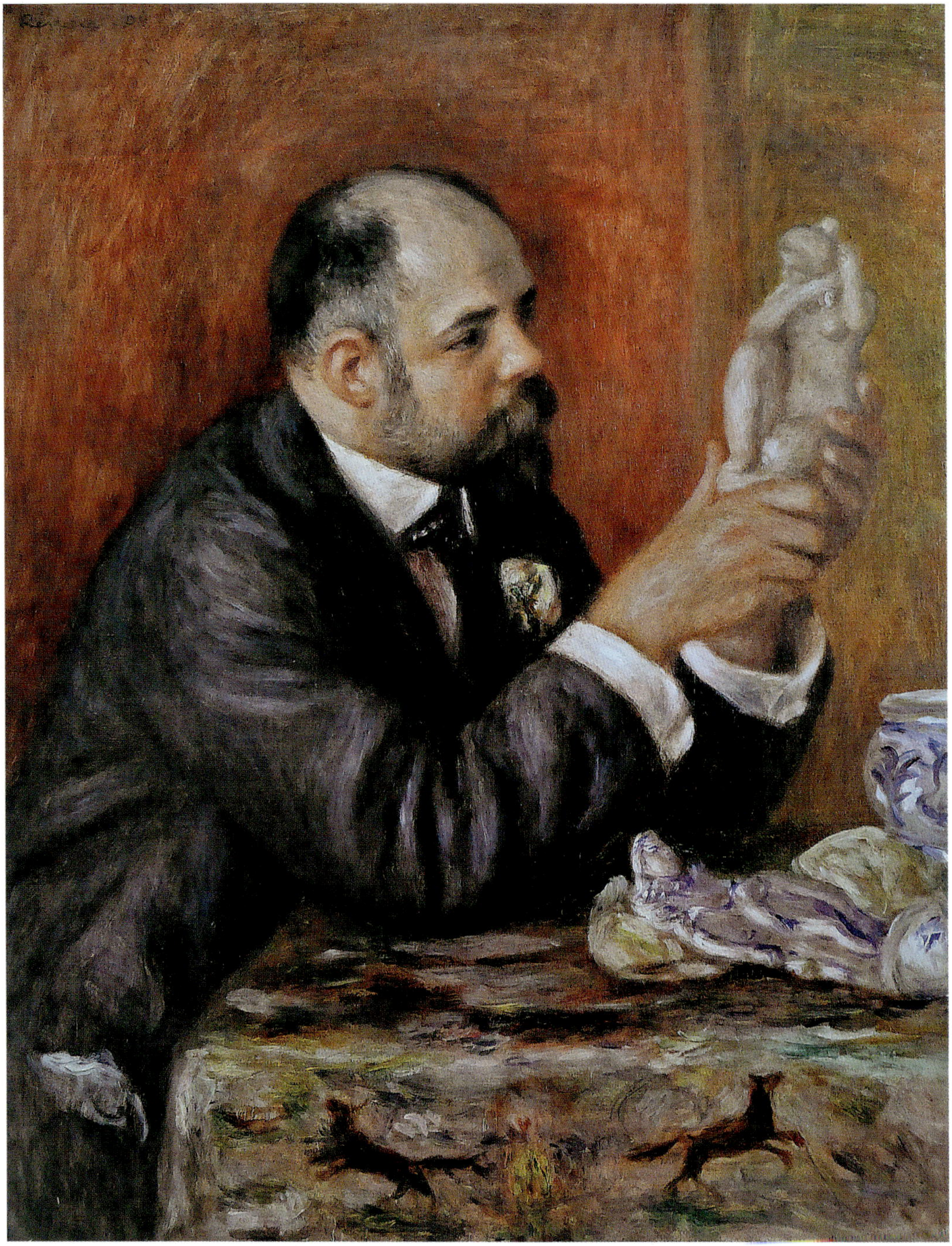

Portrait of Vollard, 1908

him to dwell upon the intoxicating dream of an imagined classical past, where man and woman lived in harmony and plenitude in a warm protective paradise. As the indignities of invalidism encroached, art transported Renoir to a primordial Eden as he abandoned himself to the liberation of pure desire detached from critical distance and narrative. In this late Rose period, Renoir found in the female nude a subject that would become a conduit through which he could express all that was important to him.

Renoir's strategy of exhibiting with avant-garde groups as well as also submitting to the Salon continued through the 1890s and 1900s. (He exhibited in the Salon up to 1912.) Throughout the 1900s and 1910s appreciation for Renoir increased among the public. He was awarded the Legion d'Honneur in 1900. Large solo exhibitions were held in Paris, New York and London; museums sought to acquire major early pieces for their collections. The first monograph on the artist appeared in 1911, first in German, with a French edition following the next year. American millionaire Albert C. Barnes began to buy what would amount to an outstanding collection of Renoirs, eventually totalling 181 pictures, many of them major works. His collection included decorative works, such as *Caryatids* (c. 1910) (page 29).

The frail artist was escorted between residences in Paris, Essoyes and Cagnes. His final journey abroad took place in 1910 to Munich, at the invitation of a collector. By the 1910s Renoir's infirmity had become so severe he was unable to walk. He became severely underweight and suffered chronic weakness. So deformed and inarticulate did his hands become that paintbrushes had to be placed in them

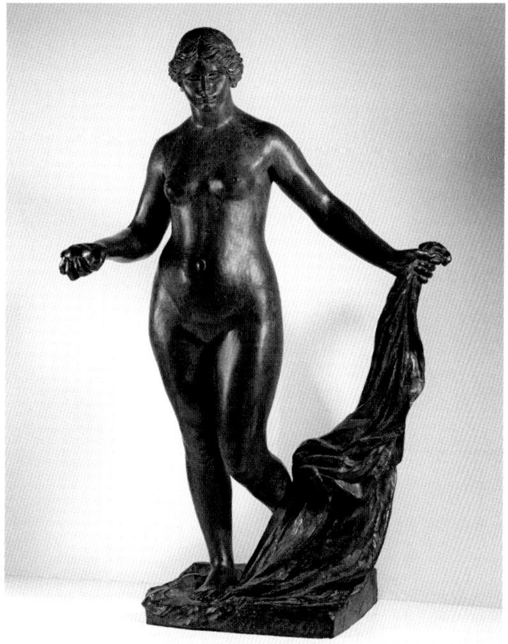

Pierre-Auguste Renoir and Richard Guino, *Venus Victorious*, 1914

by others. All remarked on how Renoir remained alert and positive despite the now constant pain. The artist's dedication to his art never wavered; he was remarkably productive in his last decades. In the remaining years of Renoir's life, painting and supporting his children gave him the will to live despite persistent discomfort and the constraints of invalidism. In conversation, Renoir rejected art that described autobiographically the artist's suffering, instead preferring art that was reticent and detached.

Aristide Maillol paid a visit to Renoir, at the behest of their mutual dealer Vollard, to sculpt a bust, probably in 1907 (or possibly 1906). Starting in 1914, consecutive collaborations with three sculptors allowed Renoir to translate figures into clay then into bronze. Too weak and immobile to perform the labour himself, Renoir instructed assistants on

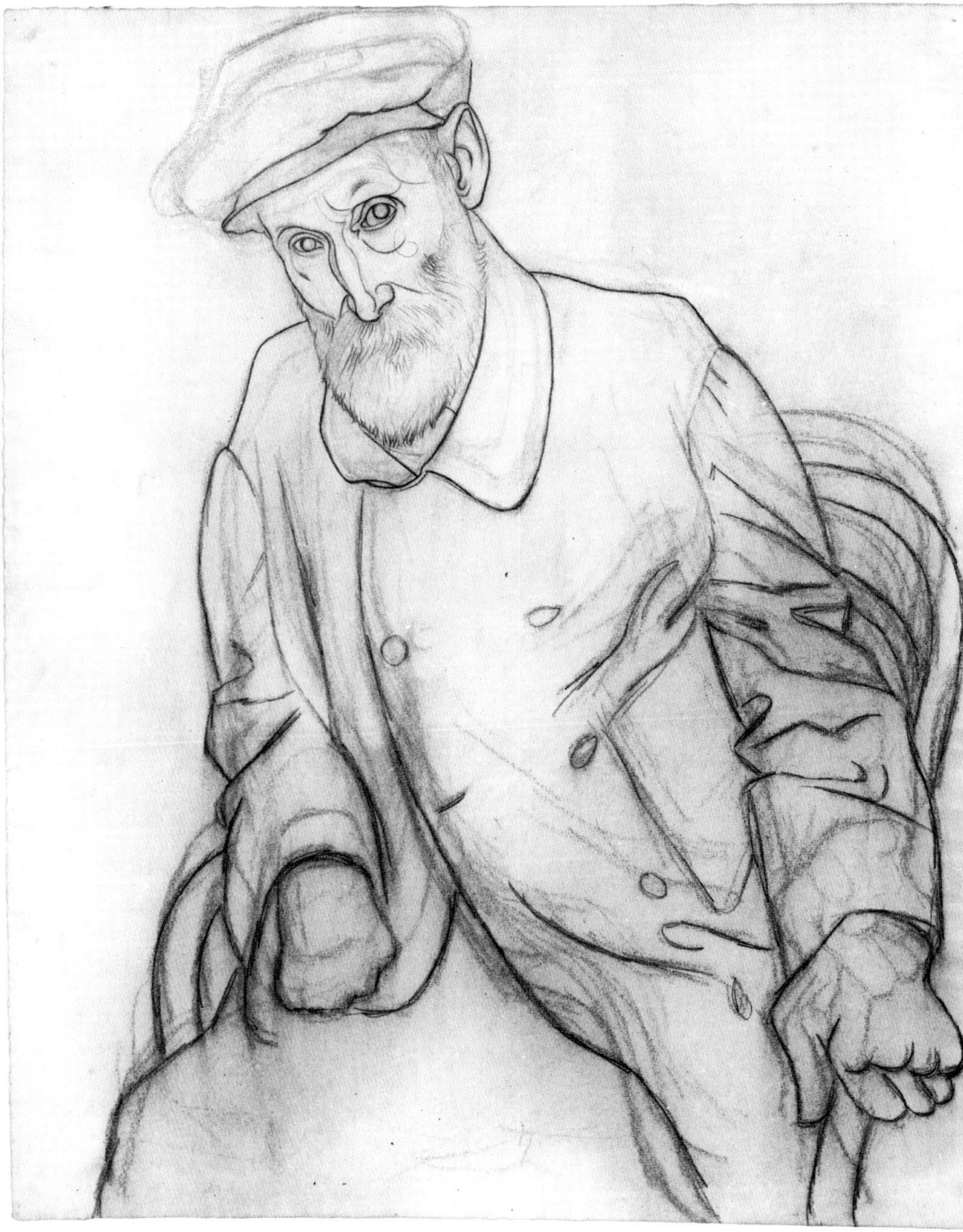

Pablo Picasso, *Portrait of Renoir*, 1919

turning motifs into sculpture, giving guidance at every stage. *Venus Victorious* (1914) is as much a tribute to French Baroque sculpture as it is to ancient Greek statuary. Apparently, Renoir claimed that the greatest living sculptor was Degas. This is an interesting comment, as Degas exhibited only one sculpture in his lifetime. The comment reveals Renoir's familiarity with Degas's small clay and wax statuettes of women and horses, which he must have seen firsthand in Degas's studio. They would be made public after Degas's death in September 1917. In 1914 Renoir oversaw production of his own designs by the Gobelins tapestry factory.

Renoir's concern for his eldest sons (who saw active combat service in the Great War) would be partially alleviated by these endeavours. In 1914 Gabrielle would leave the Renoir household and marry. During the winter of 1915/6, Renoir, in need of constant inspiration and companionship, took Catherine "Dédée" Hessling (born Andrée Heuschling) (1900–1979) as his final model. On 27 June 1915, while Jean and Pierre were recovering from war injuries, their mother Aline—taxed by years of ill-health and worried about her sons—died at home. The relationship between Aline and Renoir had been strained for years. Madame Renoir's dismissal of Gabrielle (model, secretary and nurse) had seriously isolated and distressed Renoir. Differing aspirations and needs of the couple meant that initial closeness had, by the end of their marriage, become estrangement.

Renoir died peacefully on the evening of 3 December 1919 at his home, with his family beside him. Huge public affection for his art, and the respect of fellow artists, was evident in the tributes that subsequently followed. In April 1921, a Paris exhibition of 156 works on paper by Renoir presented an overlooked aspect of his oeuvre. Artists as diverse as de Chirico, Picasso, Matisse and others took up Renoir as a hero during the *rappel à l'ordre* (Fr: call to order) revival of classicism in the 1920s and 1930s. Picasso made a powerful portrait of the master in the year of his death, based on a photograph (page 32). Magritte would adopt Renoir as his antidote to the doleful atmosphere of occupied Belgium during World War II. For younger advanced artists who feared art might have reached a deadening limit in arid abstraction, harsh geometry and intellectualism, Renoir—whose pictures were dedicated to simple pleasures, immersion in the senses and the foundational principle of irregularity—would become their guiding star.

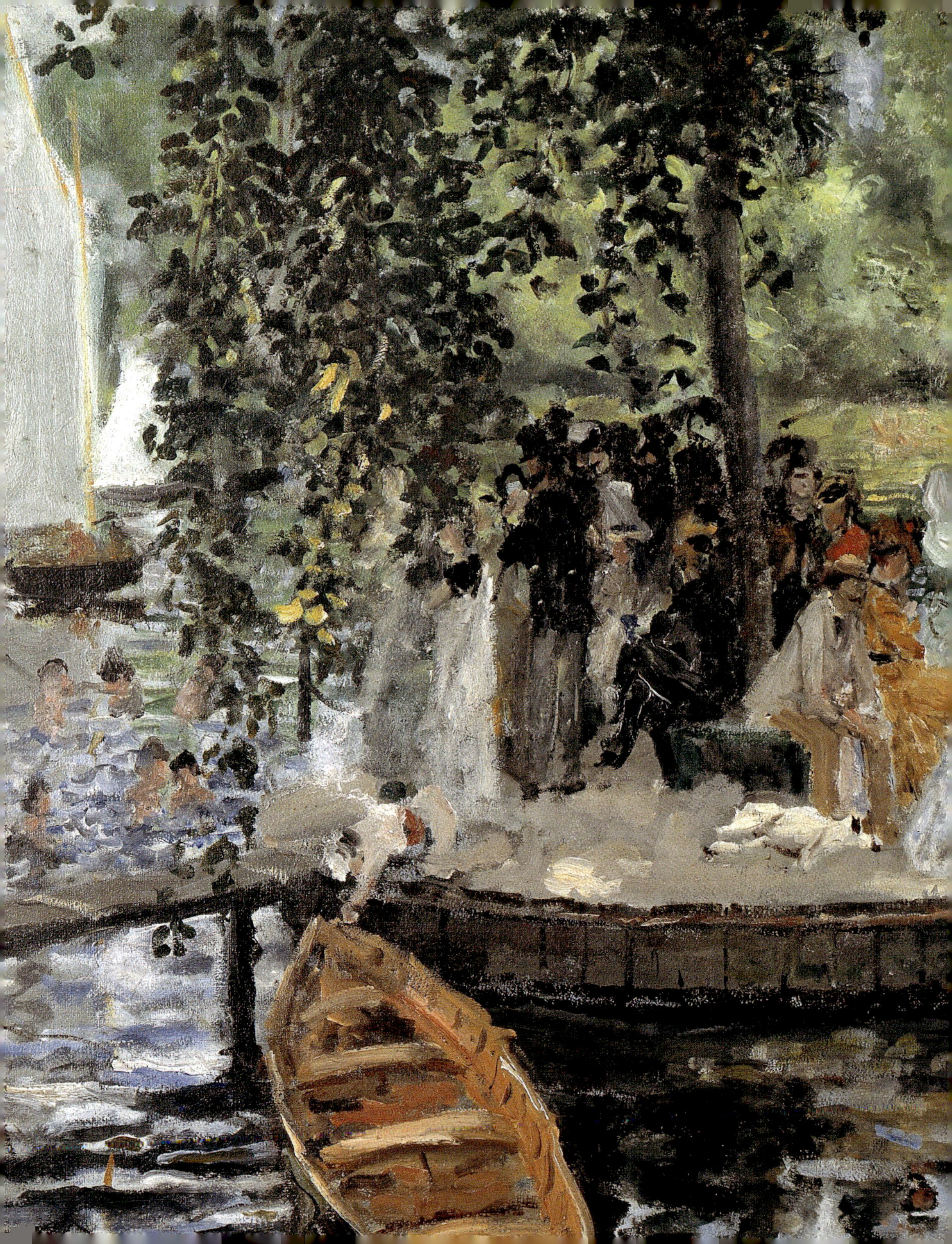

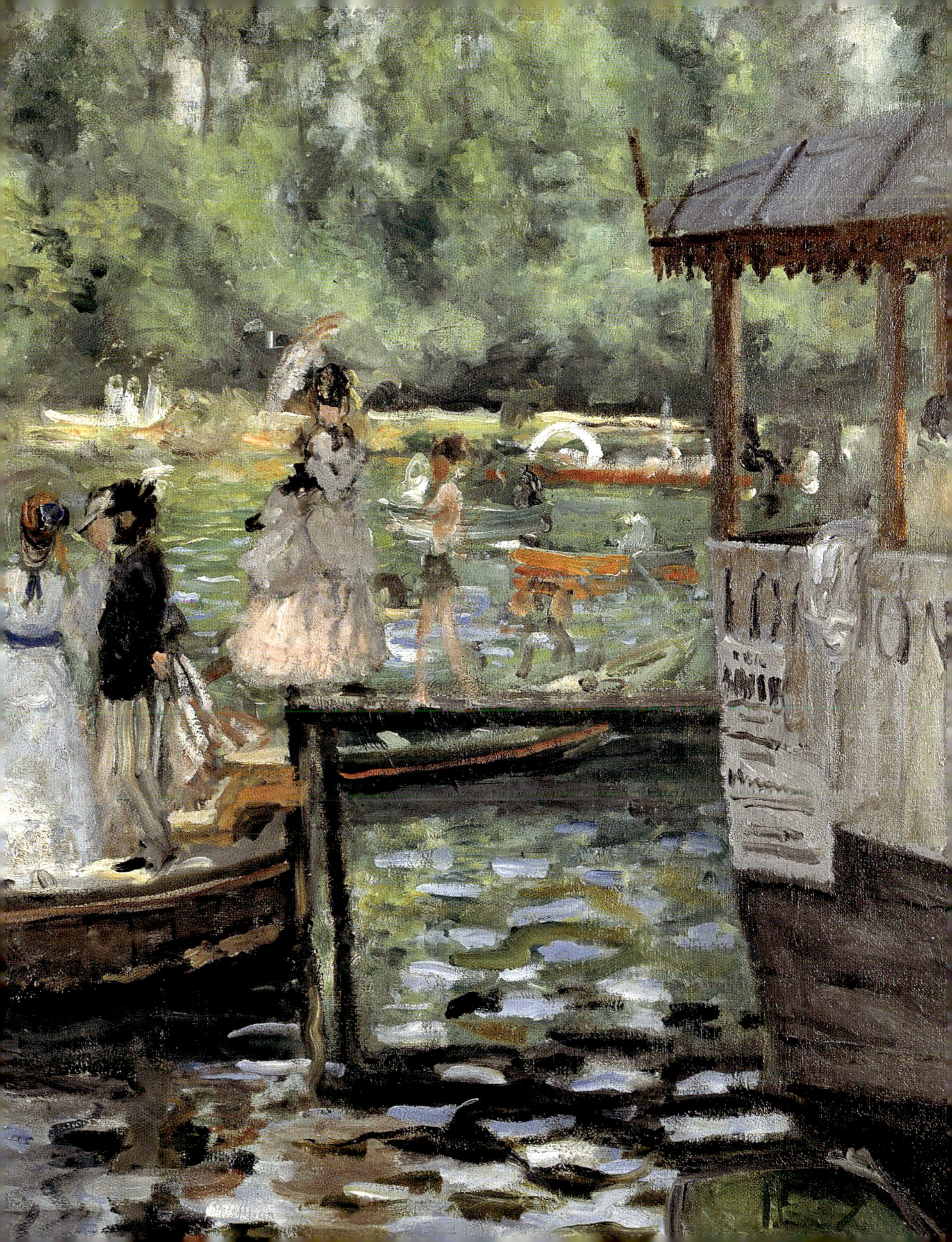

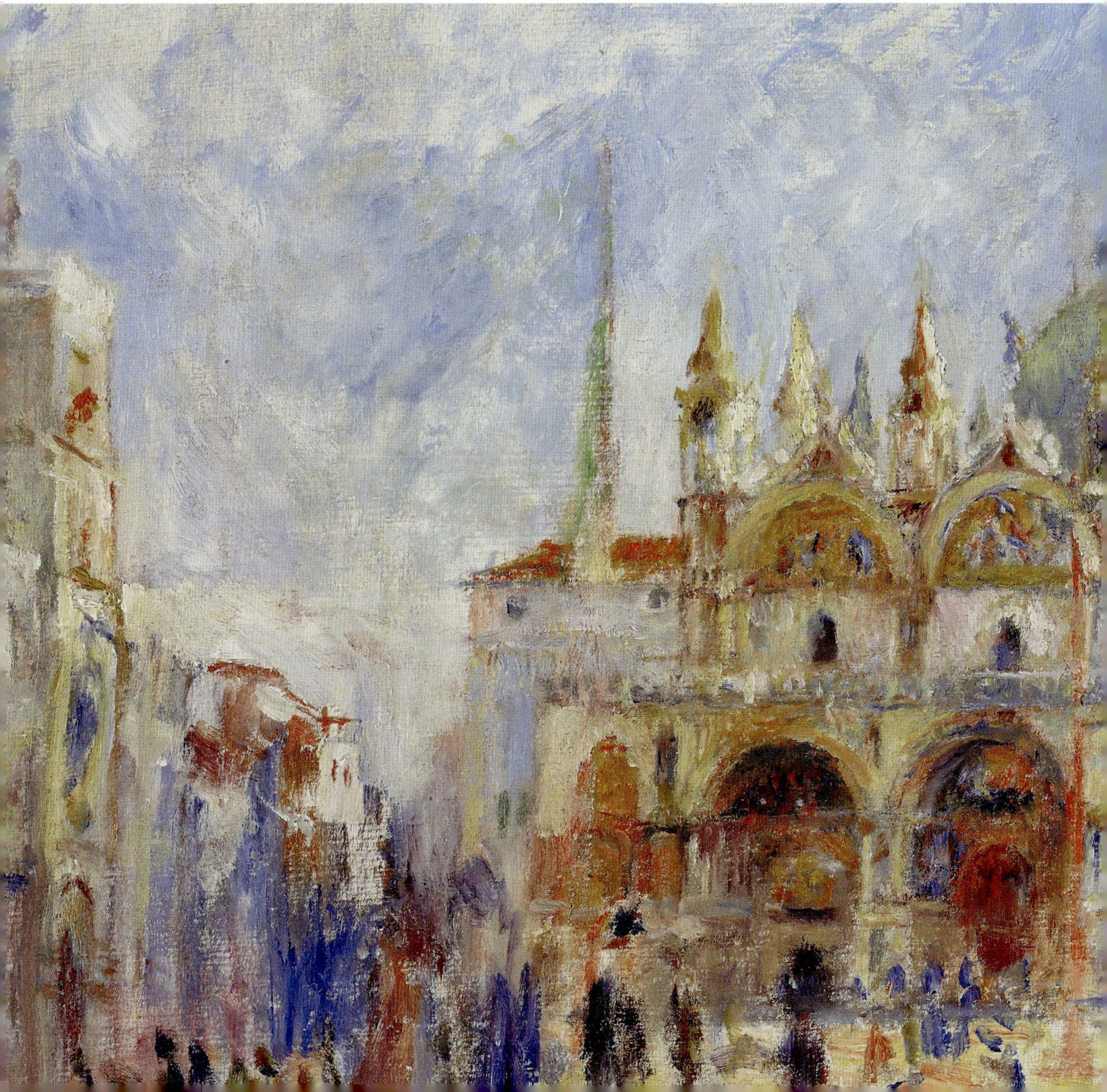

WORKS

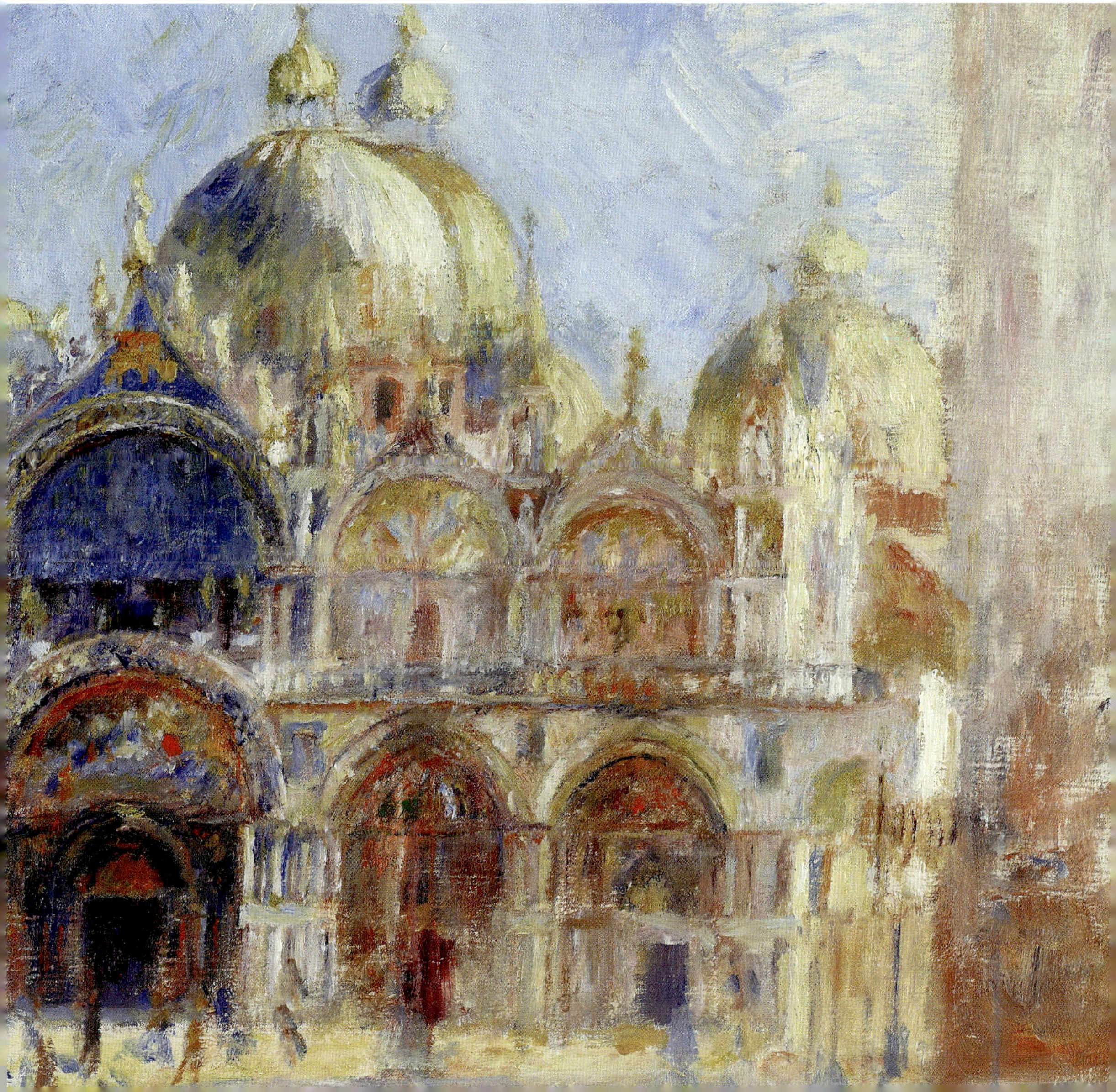

Spring Bouquet, 1866

Oil on canvas
74.9 × 55.4 cm
Fogg Museum, Harvard University

Although playing a secondary role, paintings of flowers and fruit still-lifes can be found in all of Renoir's periods. We tend to associate Renoir with the painting of flowers in situ, on the trees and bushes where they grow in wild or cultivated spaces. Rather than concentrating on the colour of the flowers, here Renoir harmonises the white roses with a white tablecloth, with a simple glazed vase providing the contrast of a dark, hard, reflective surface that heightens the softness of the petals, leaves and cloth.
A background of graduated grey encloses the bouquet, giving us the impression of a solid object in a hollow space, while not interfering with the white-green-black palette.
This still-life of flowers has a crisp modernity to it that makes it comparable to bouquets painted by Henri Fantin-Latour at about this time. Fantin-Latour and Renoir were both members of Manet's circle (page 12) and Renoir knew the former's pictures.
An additional comparison can be made between this and the flower and fruit still-lifes that Manet would create in the 1880s, at the end of his life, which echo Fantin-Latour's restrained colour harmonies and modern atmosphere.
Boucher, Watteau and Fragonard all treated flowers and greenery as essential components in settings for scenes of idyllic tristes. Critics have noted that Renoir's scenes of social and romantic encounters—from all his periods—echo those *fêtes galantes*, the genre Watteau developed as a form of courtly art. The motifs he painted at the porcelain factory were apparently figures, fruit and flowers, in the French Rococo style. Renoir also venerated Delacroix, who—aside from being a great painter of history, portraits and landscapes—was a notable flower painter.

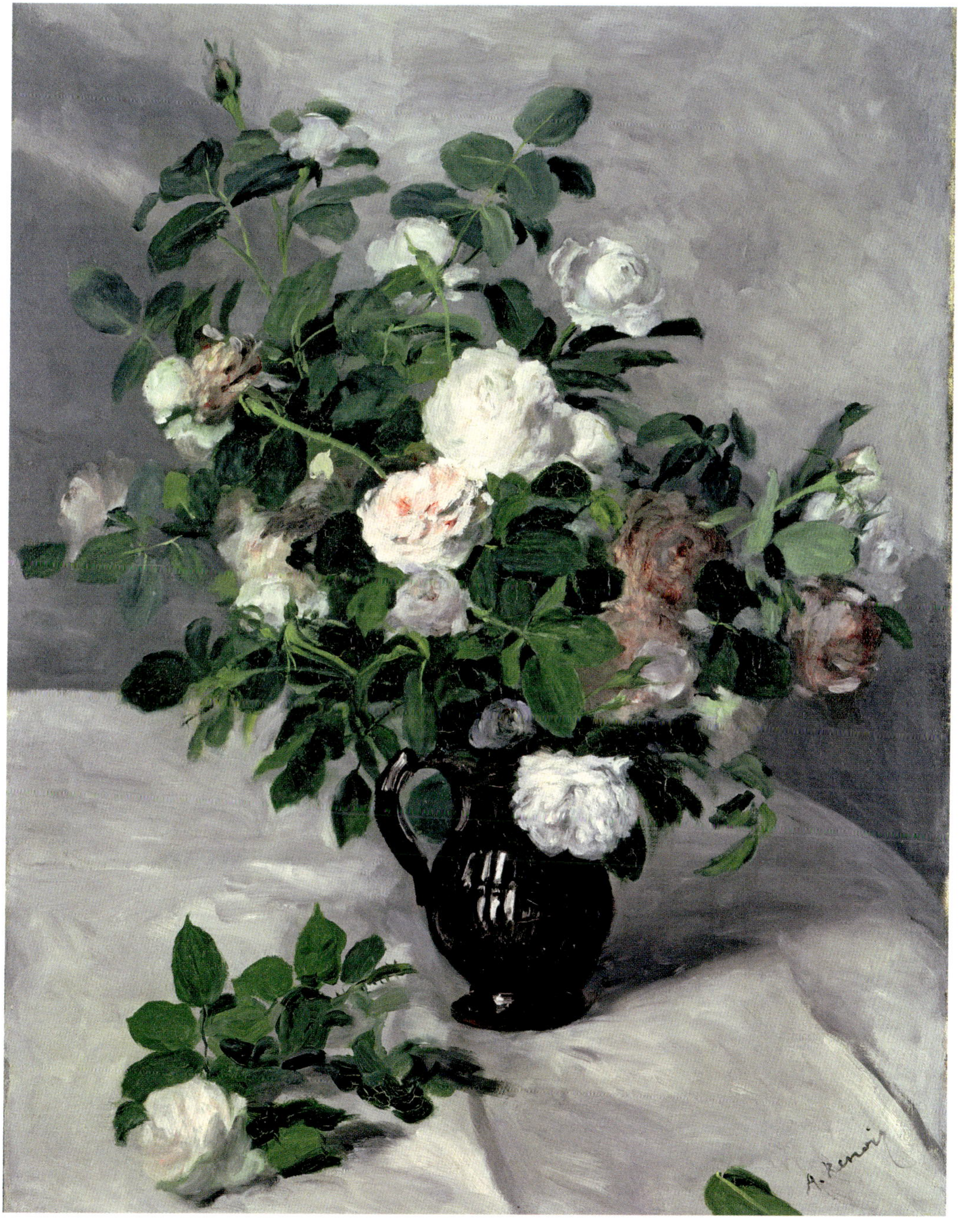

Frédéric Bazille, 1867

Oil on canvas
105 × 73.5 cm
Musée d'Orsay, Paris

Born into a family of prosperous vintners from the Midi in southern France, Frédéric Bazille was perhaps the closest early friend of Renoir. They worked side by side first in Gleyre's atelier, then in shared lodgings and studios and became trusting confidants. We have letters they exchanged and paintings they made of each other. A painting by Bazille shows their shared studio in Rue de la Condamine, including paintings on the wall by Renoir that Renoir would later destroy. They also shared models (page 12). Renoir keenly felt the loss of his colleague, even at the end of his life.
Bazille was a skillful painter, who was still developing at the time of his early death. His style was close to Manet's in terms of descriptive tightness and strong, relatively unmodulated colour. In that respect, Bazille's painting was similar to Monet's and, to a lesser extent, Renoir's in the late 1860s. Continued interest in the Impressionists has meant that Bazille's paintings are studied and appreciated to this day, despite his potential being cut short. Stylistically, Bazille's paintings had not developed into classic Impressionism by the time of his death.
This painting belonged to Monet. After Bazille's death it was acquired by the subject's father, who exchanged another painting for it. It was loaned for inclusion in the second Independent exhibition in 1876—obviously a tribute to a colleague who would (had he lived) undoubtedly have joined the Impressionist group. This painting was presented to the French state in 1923 by the Bazille family.

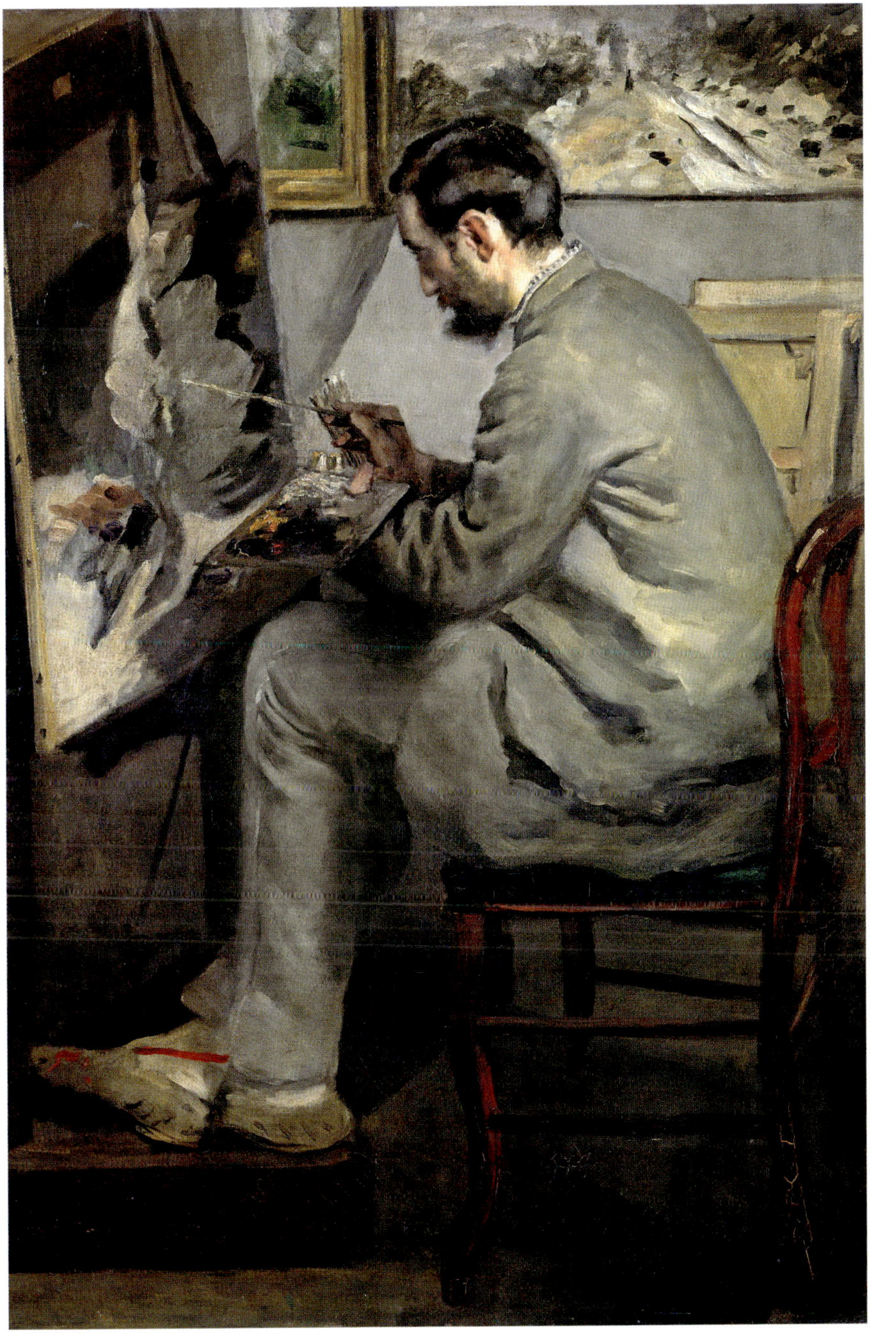

Diana, 1867

Oil on canvas
199.5 × 129.5 cm
National Gallery of Art, Washington DC

"Renoir has painted an extraordinary picture, which has astonished everyone", Bazille wrote to his mother on 20 March 1867 about this painting. It depicts Diana, Roman goddess of nature and the moon in her role as goddess of the hunt; she rests on a rock, contemplating a slain deer. Although painted in the studio, Renoir has convincingly described the quality of sunlight bathing the figure.

Diana was an impressive performance for a young artist, nonetheless it was rejected by the Salon jury of 1867. Jury members likely sensed that the goddess Diana as a huntress was merely a pretext for the naturalistic depiction of a very real body (in this case Lise's). It would be uncomfortably and recognisably truthful for an audience and therefore might cause embarrassment.

Renoir was well acquainted with art about Diana in the Louvre collection, including a famous painting of Diana produced by the Mannerist School of Fontainebleau. Renoir's Diana is inspired by more modern precedents. *Diana* is painted in the spirit of Courbet, whose groundbreaking depictions of actual women in outdoor settings had caused a sensation over the 1850s and 1860s. Not just the style—including colour choices and use of palette knife—but the large size, vertical format and prominence of the figure also followed Courbet's lead. Courbet had received acclaim and notoriety for his large nudes, only begrudgingly accepted by the Salon jury. This imitation must have seemed too blatant. The rejection of *Diana* may have contributed to Renoir's move to establish his independence from Courbet by taking up urban views and scenes of leisure and embracing the advances of Monet and Pissarro, which came to be called Impressionism.

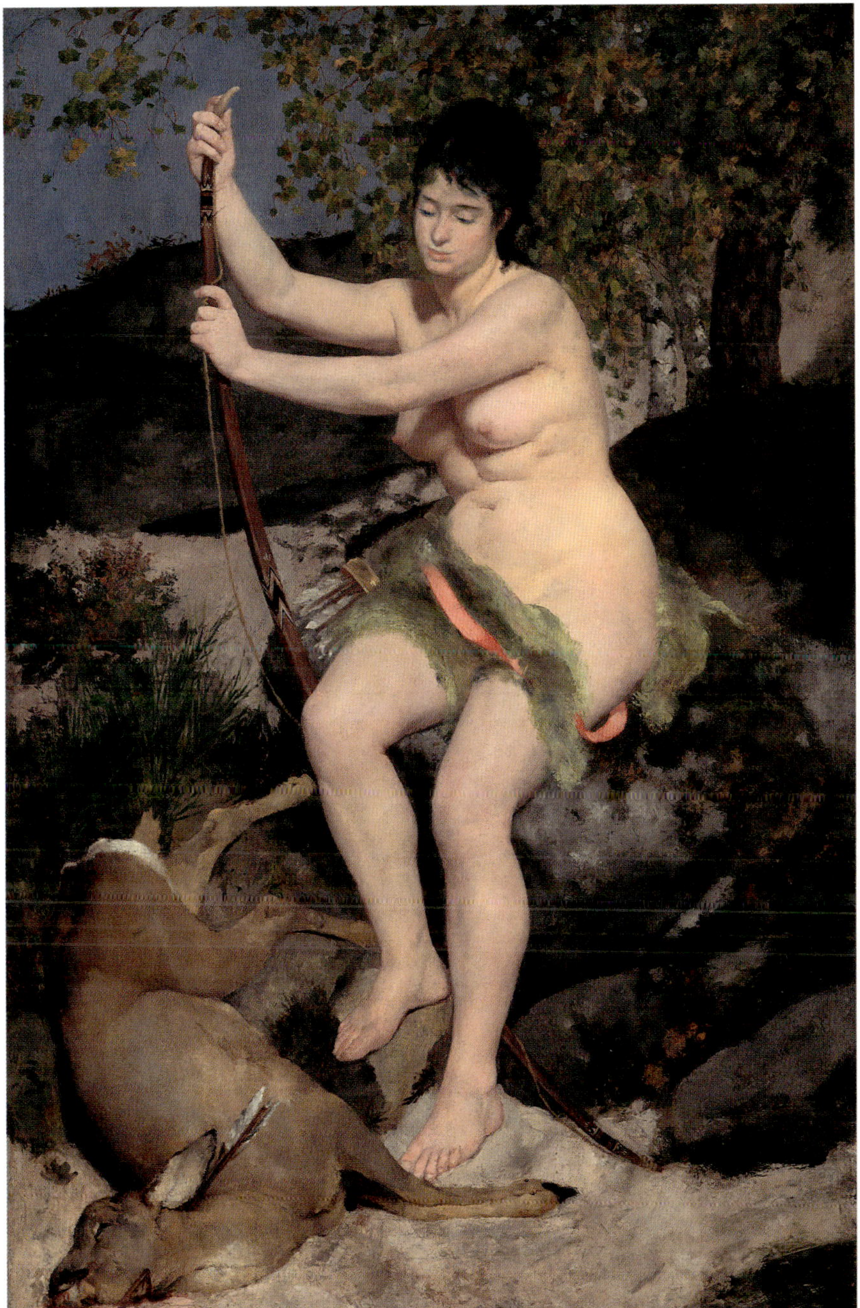

The Pont des Arts, Paris, 1867/8

Oil on canvas
60.9 × 100.3 cm
Norton Simon Museum, Pasadena

The clarity and precision of this early cityscape remind us of Renoir's contemporaneous engagement with the School of Barbizon. Noted for naturalism, detail and immediacy, those painters inspired the Impressionists and prompted them to paint in the landscape. The adoption of accurate colours and light effects went against the teaching of Gleyre and the École des Beaux-Arts. Although students were encouraged to study nature, it was only intended to be a guide and to assist in the creation of persuasive artificial scenes of a mythological, religious or historical character. For the Barbizon and Impressionist painters, nature itself was a suitable subject for "finished" art.

The chimney shadows in the lower area direct our attention to the centre of the picture, which is located at the apex of the squat triangle of sunlit ground. The wide format is an interesting choice. Wide canvases were called "marines" by colourmen (material suppliers of the time who were also manufacturers, making canvases to size for example) and painters, as they were commonly used for sea paintings and, less often, for panoramic landscapes. Daubigny (of the Barbizon School) was well known for his use of the double-square (1:2) format. It was rare for the Batignolles Group—and later the Impressionists—to use emphatically horizontal formats, which indicates Renoir's individualism in his selection of this format, chosen from a colourman's catalogue of standard sizes of pre-stretched canvas. In later years, Renoir would pin canvas directly to the studio wall and only mount it on a stretcher after the picture was finished.

This canvas was bought from the artist's studio by Durand-Ruel on 16 March 1872 for the low price of 200 francs, indicating the lack of a market for Renoir's paintings that were not portraits.

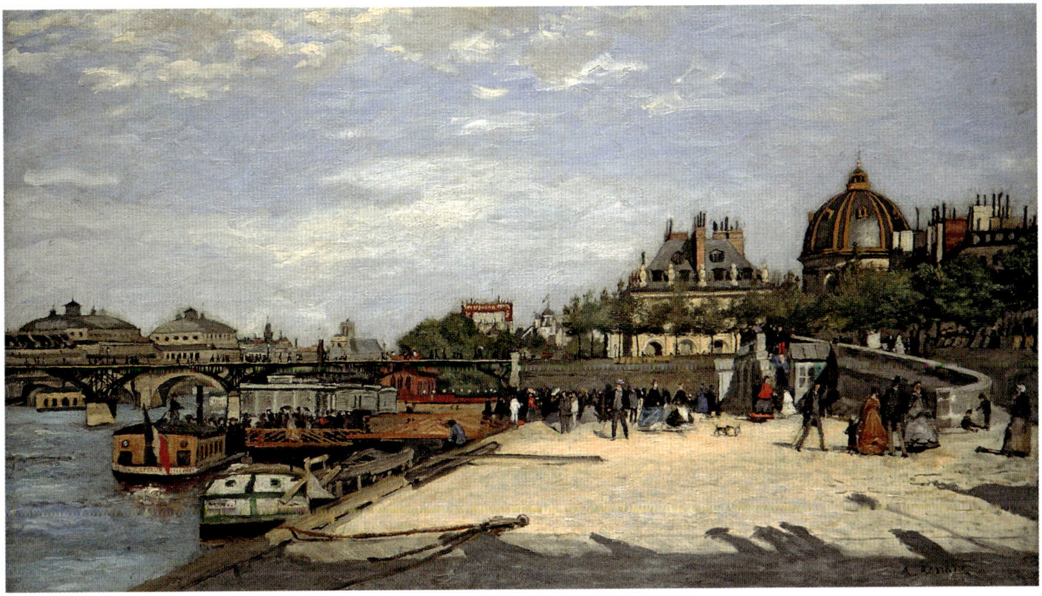

In Summer, 1868

Oil on canvas
85 × 59 cm
Alte Nationalgalerie, Berlin

For Renoir, simplicity and lack of affectation were the key to grace in life and beauty in art. The model here is Lise, depicted as especially youthful considering her actual age of 20 years. The tightness of drawing comes from years of life-classes and the legacy of executing precision work in the porcelain factory. The freshness of the model's appearance is increased by the rich verdancy of the background—a harbinger of Impressionist brushwork. The apparent vulnerability of the young woman—evident in the looseness of her clothing and dreamy distracted gaze —display tenderness towards Lise; one wonders how different their subsequent lives might have been had Renoir been sufficiently financially stable to marry her.
The tonal range is quite dramatic, partly as a consequence of Manet's example. Stripes would be an important decorative element for Renoir. Although they were common in fabric at the time, Renoir particularly delighted in the use of bold pattern, as seen in *A Couple* (page 49), which he used to provide animating contrast and direct the gaze. The warmth of the day is conveyed through use of small dabbed and blurred strokes. The shimmer of heat haze, fluctuating shadow and dazzle are well conveyed by Renoir's innovative paint handling. The artist retained a relatively simple palette of lead white, Naples yellow, yellow ochre, burnt sienna, carmine, venetian red, madder red, scarlet vermilion, crimson lake, emerald green, Veronese green, cobalt blue and ivory black. He preferred chrome yellow and cobalt blue in his Realist and Impressionist years; Naples yellow and French ultramarine are found in his paintings from the early 1880s onwards; he did not use Prussian blue or cadmium yellow. Unlike the other Impressionists, Renoir often exploited glazes (page 26).

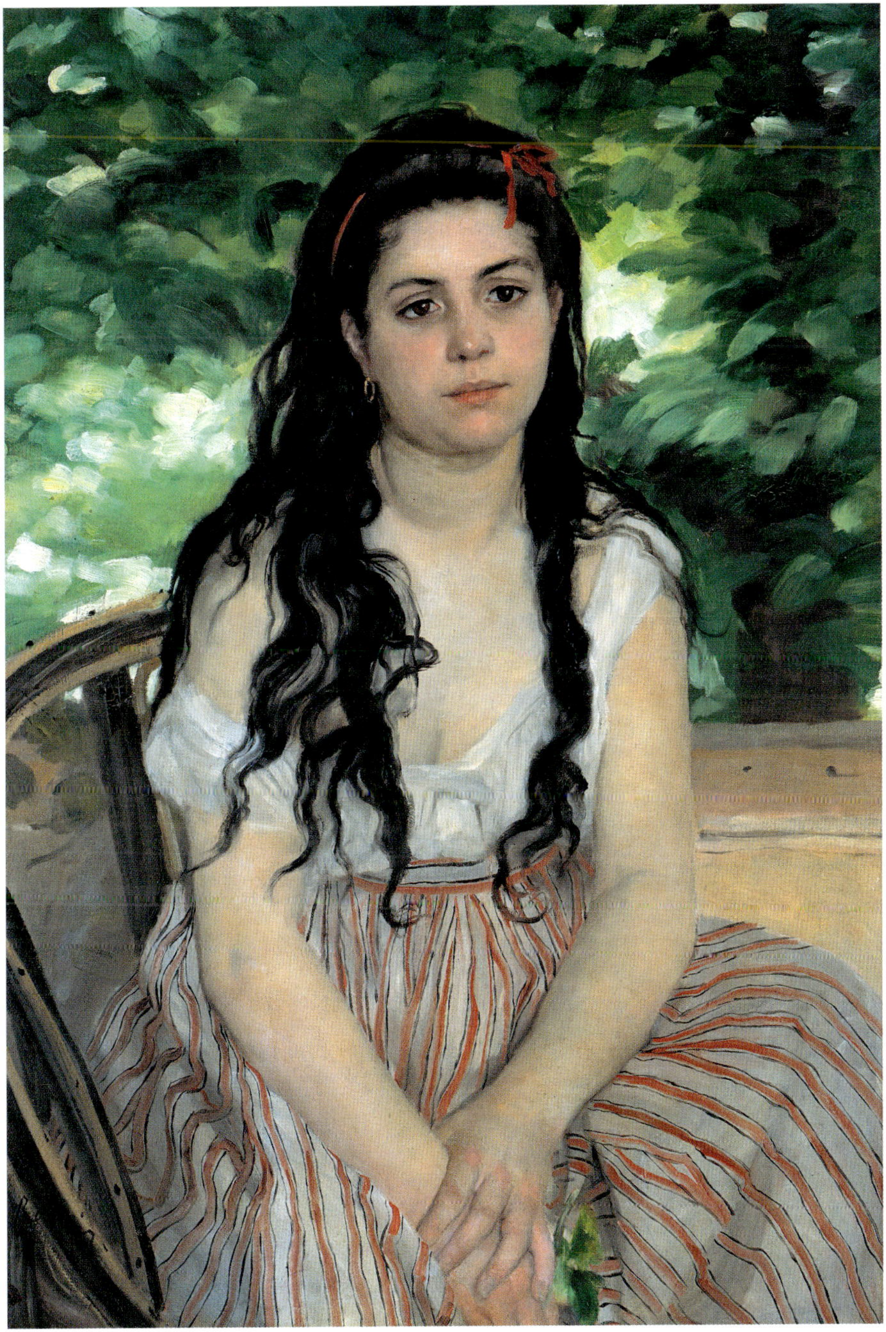

A Couple, 1868

Oil on canvas
105 × 75 cm
Wallraf-Richartz Museum, Cologne

Previously misidentified as being a portrait of Sisley and his wife, this painting is now largely agreed by scholars to be of Sisley with Lise, Renoir's mistress and model. Renoir mentioned in personal notes a double portrait of the pair. This woman looks almost identical to Lise (as seen in other paintings of this time) and decidedly different from Eugénie "Marie" Sisley née Lescouezec (1834–1898), who was blonde. In the later dance paintings of 1883, Renoir would pair models according to their appearance and character rather than relying upon pre-existing connections between models. So, this pairing is not out of character for Renoir, whose primary concern was with pictorial strength rather than biographical veracity.

As in *In Summer* (page 47), the background is deliberately indistinct, which directs our attention to the subject and heightens the impression of clarity. This is a key aspect of Impressionism, which is the first style that emerged following widespread exposure to photography. Due to lens-derived imagery presenting areas of focus and non-focus, artists had "objective" proof of how clarity and indistinctness affect perception, as subsequently developed in their painting. The harmony of gold and scarlet stripes provides a scintillating area of rippling pattern that provides a foil to the blacks, greens and earth hues.

Very much a specialist in landscape, Sisley was one of the Batignolles Group and a founder member of the Impressionists. Sisley's English nationality meant that he was not drafted during the French-Prussian War. He never achieved the level of success of his colleagues during his lifetime, living largely in poverty.

Picasso was beguiled by this painting (then called *Sisley and his Wife*) and he drew several copies. Newly married in 1919, Picasso perhaps saw the couple as emblematic of the ideal happily married artist and spouse.

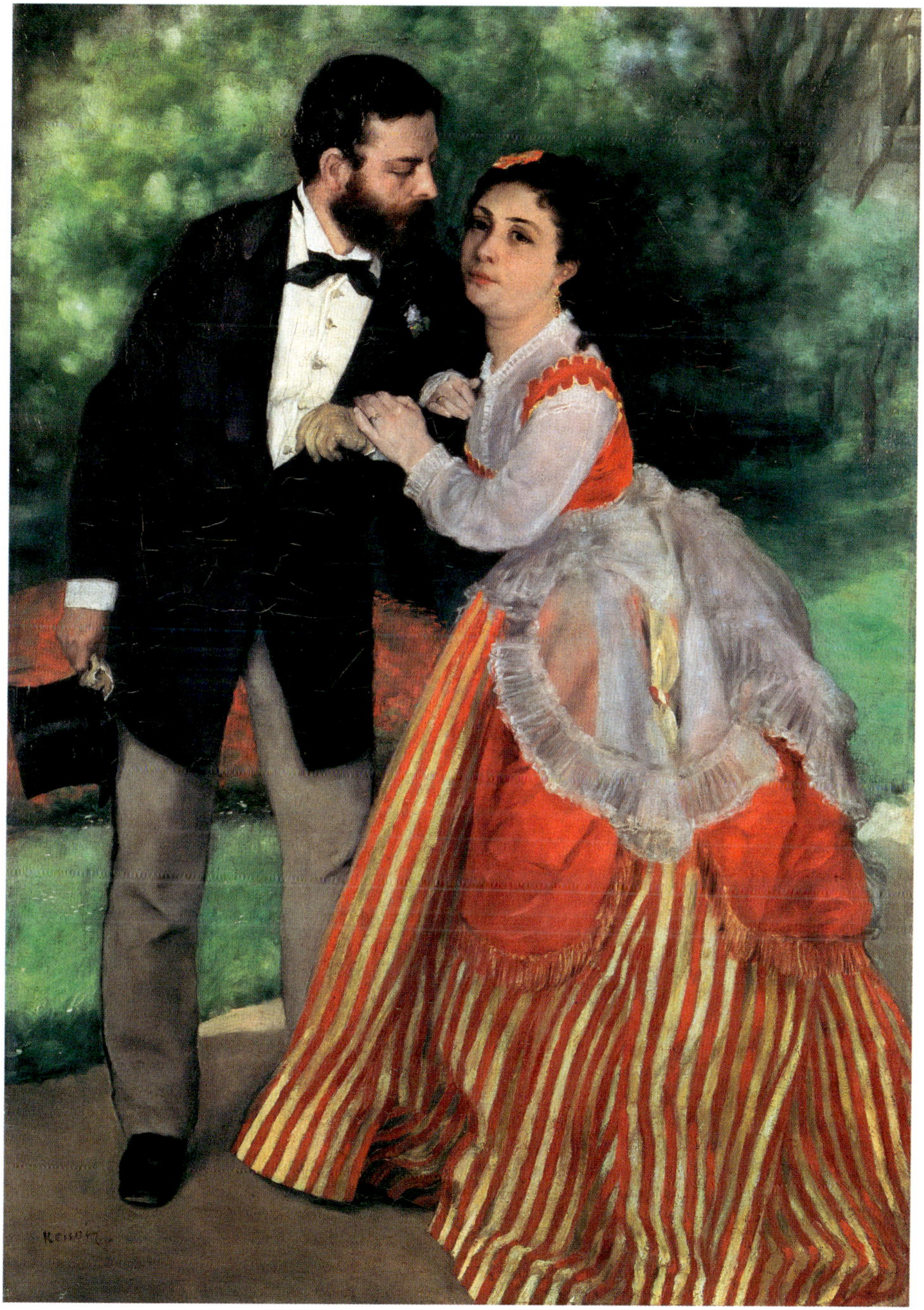

Le Grenouillère, 1869

Oil on canvas
66.5 × 81 cm
Nationalmuseum, Stockholm

According to a letter from Monet to Bazille, six test paintings by Monet and Renoir of this motif had been finished by 25 September 1869. (Of which two by each of the artists have been located.) The intention was to make more finished paintings for the 1869 Salon.
The pair selected as a location Le Grenouillère, a popular boating and picnicking spot on the Seine, named after the frogs that inhabited the banks. Monet, who had previously worked there, invited Renoir to paint beside him. This was one of fourteen established instances of Renoir and Monet painting the landscape side by side.
The initial sketches executed on the spot did not prompt Renoir to develop a larger painting, as they were suitably smooth and consistent in detail and *facture* (Fr: surface) for the Salon jury. It would be the six *ébauches* (Fr: painted sketches), made so hastily in order to capture moving figures and changing light conditions, that laid the groundwork for the Impressionist style. The very qualities that made them inappropriate for Salon juries—minimal detail, rough and visible brushwork, contrast of smooth paintwork and thick impasto, dramatically broken areas of colour, and unfinished character—made them exciting and engaging in themselves. The painters found that such directness gave pictures immediacy and energy. They also believed that if they recorded appearances in an optical way that approximated how people actually see, this would be an insight into human experience. For precedent, they referred back to the Venetian masters, as well as to Delacroix and Turner.
The other picture of this subject by Renoir is in the Oskar Reinhart Collection "Am Römerholz", Winterthur. The Stockholm painting is unsigned, which indicates that Renoir at this time did not consider it finished or significant. In contrast to Renoir, Monet decided to translate his sketches into a large presentation-quality oil painting, which is now lost.
Le Grenouillère is located near the village of Bougival, where Renoir would situate *Dance at Bougival* (page 87).

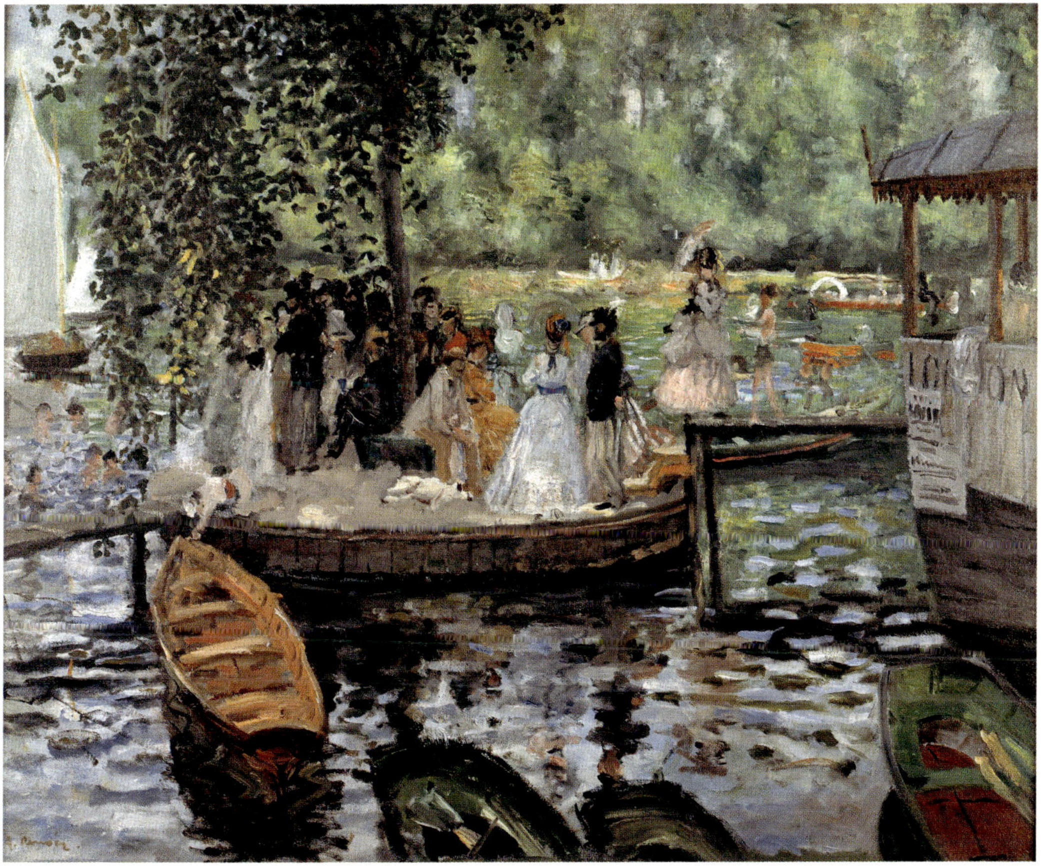

Odalisque, 1870

Oil on canvas
69.2 × 122.6 cm
National Gallery of Art, Washington DC

The odalisque was a popular archetype of nineteenth-century painting, especially in France. It presents the female figure, draped or nude, in an exotic setting conveying the indolence, decadence and strangeness of the Orient. The School of Batignolles greatly admired Delacroix's orientalist scenes. Although some European artists visited North Africa, the Near or Far East to document actual or staged scenes—including the odalisque—it was common for painters to fabricate in their studios *mises en scenes*, using models, clothing and props. It became fashionable for Europeans to have themselves painted in oriental garb.

This painting was exhibited at the 1870 Salon where it attracted some praise for the artist's skill in depicting fabrics. The same year, Bazille would paint Lise standing in an oriental gown, in his masterpiece *La Toilette* (1869/70), which is a harem scene rich in colour and depicted texture, where a nude woman is being dressed by assistants. The figure on the right, in a striped dress, is Lise.

In the 1870s, Renoir would be commissioned to copy Delacroix's *Jewish Wedding* (1839), which is set in Tangiers. In 1881 and 1882 he would have the chance to visit French North Africa to compare reality with the orientalist paintings he was familiar with from the Louvre collection and the annual Salon. Traditional moral codes meant that Renoir did not have access to female models there. Disappointed, the best he could manage was a few hasty sketches of clothed figures on the street. Renoir's few paintings from Algeria are principally landscapes and buildings, an outdoor crowd scene, portraits and interiors. Ultimately, the painter's interest in the Orient would diminish, as he found contemplation of Old Masters and ancient art more congenial.

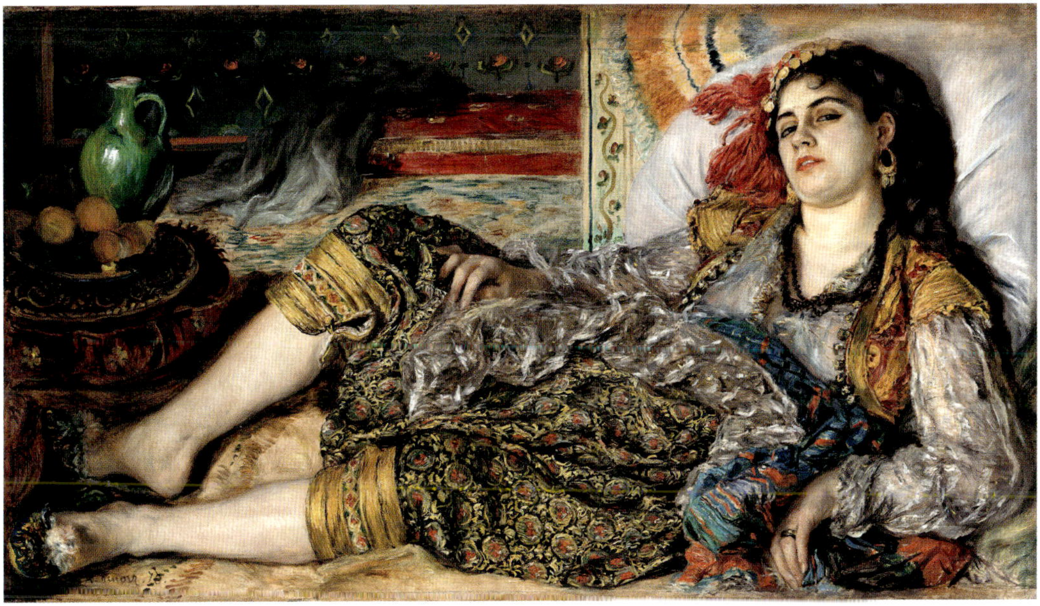

Pont Neuf, Paris, 1872

Oil on canvas
75.3 × 93.7 cm
National Gallery of Art, Washington DC

Built at the end of the sixteenth century, Pont Neuf (New Bridge) links two banks of the Seine to the tip of the Île de la Cité and is the oldest surviving bridge in Paris; it is instantly recognisable to Parisians. Here, the grand orderly architecture of the bridge sets off the picturesque vernacular of the mismatched house façades. The sturdiness of the bridge contrasts with the flow of traffic and its fleeting figures. Renoir (at an upper-storey window) apparently entrusted Edmond to detain pedestrians in conversation long enough for the painter to covertly sketch them.

The Impressionists—especially Gustave Caillebotte, Monet and Pissarro—painted street scenes, documenting urban life in the metropolis. They depicted modern forms of Parisian transport including omnibuses and trains and the newly introduced electric street lighting, which began in 1878. At a time when Symbolist and academic art refused to address aspects of urban existence (including technology), the Impressionists displayed a frank curiosity about life, viewed at both an intimate domestic level and a distant macroscopic level. Just as the new fields of sociology and urban planning sought to explain and control human behaviour, so the Impressionists sought to record metropolitan life. The adoption of new techniques and subjects went hand in hand for these consciously groundbreaking artists.

Renoir—assisted by his brother Edmond, a professional author—wrote an article about decoration in urban architecture. It reveals how important he considered ornamentation and variation. Renoir explicitly rejected the standardisation that was a necessary aspect of Baron Haussmann's process of urbanising and modernising central Paris between 1853 and 1870. Haussmann pioneered the use of prefabricated components for those who bought dwellings off plan, likewise standardising set dimensions for ground plans, storeys, doors and windows. The variation in design and finish of individual craftsmanship was absent in Haussmann's mass-produced balustrades, door fittings and gas lamps. Renoir described himself as a craftsman rather than an intellectual. "I prefer a dull-witted artisan any day to a machine."

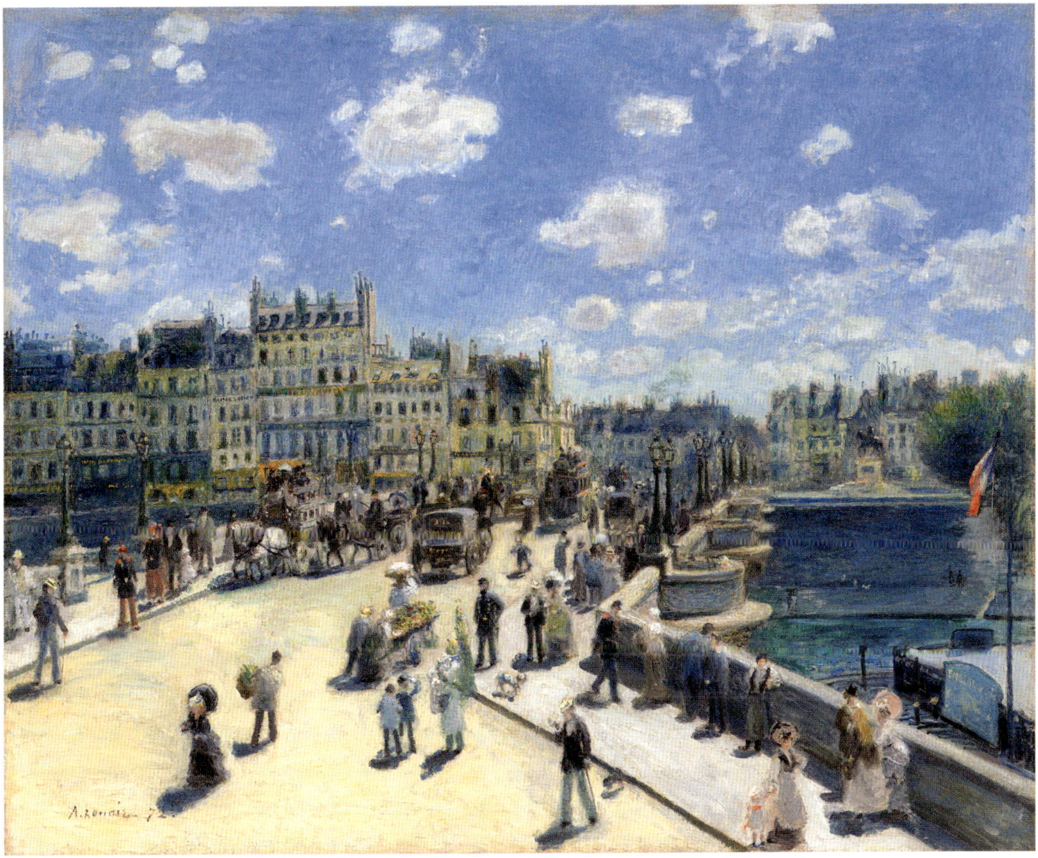

La Loge (The Theatre Box), 1874

Oil on canvas
80 × 63.5 cm
The Courtauld, London

Another painting by Renoir of this time (*At the Theatre (La Première Sortie)* (1876/7)) depicts a young lady at her first social event, presented seated in a theatre or opera box, leaning forward in anxious anticipation and absorbed by the spectacle before her. Both that composition and this are notable for their very tight cropping, which differs from the more anecdotal vignette approach used by society painters. In *La Loge*, Renoir is more interested in the visual qualities of figures—model Nini Lopez and Edmond Renoir—than establishing a narrative or engaging in social commentary.

Viewers would have been perplexed by the way the two figures seem intermingled, lacking the clear distinction usually made. Stripes push upward, directing our gaze towards the decolletage and face of the lady, which comprise a balanced vase-like form that is the heart of the composition. The rose in her hair accentuates the vase-like quality of that bright area. The colours of the minor areas of flowers, box edge and the lady's opera-glasses only emphasise that this painting is a play of black, white and cream. According to Jean Renoir, the painter said, "Black is a very important colour, perhaps the most important".

Renoir visited the opera quite often when in Paris, although he found the architecture of Paris's main opera house abominable. He had a somewhat relaxed attitude towards the experience, often enjoying looking at the concertgoers, especially the women, and finding longer performances boring. His restless energy made passive confinement a chore and he once described the reduction of light and confinement of illumination to the stage as a form of tyranny that controlled one's gaze by obscuring all else apart from the performance area.

This painting was exhibited in the first Independent (Impressionist) exhibition. When it received criticism, Renoir is supposed to have commented, "Perhaps it's vanity, but I think it's well painted". He made three other variants of this composition at a later date. This is the best known and most admired version.

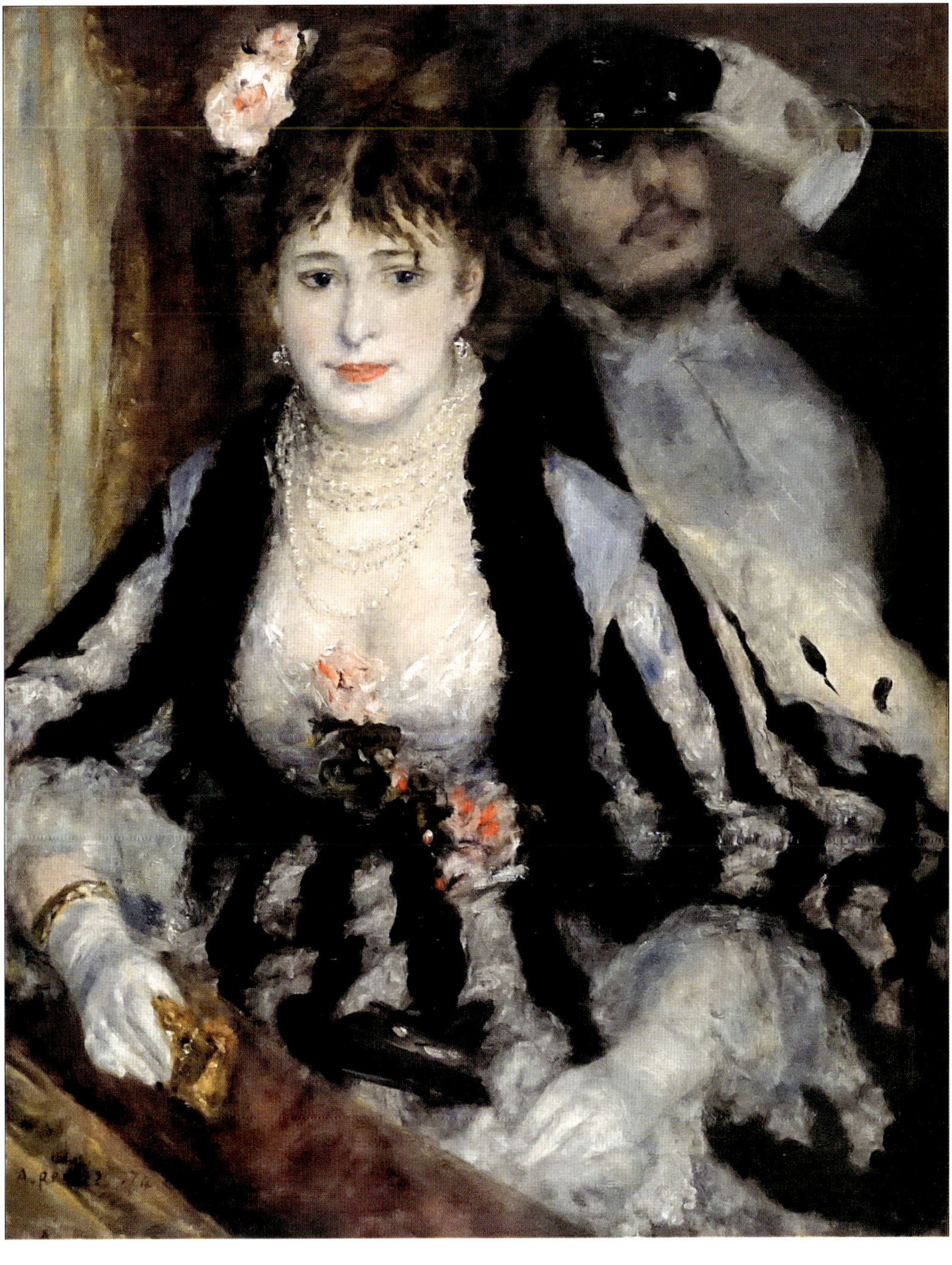

Snow-covered Landscape, c. 1875

Oil on canvas
73.5 × 89 cm
Musée d l'Orangerie, Paris

This is one of very few snowy landscapes painted by Renoir, who could not stand the cold. It is one of his most delicately painted and sensitively observed landscapes, which shows him at his closest to Pissarro. The shadows on the field of snow are scarcely less bright blue than the piercing colour of the sky. Renoir plays with pictorial depth by making a convincingly deep space but keeping the size of marks consistent between foreground and background, which conflicts with our unconscious expectation that marks for the background should be smaller than those of the foreground.

This canvas may have been painted near Monet's new house. *Frost* (1875) by Monet is almost identical in terms of motif and atmosphere to this painting, which are similar in size. It is tempting to see this as a case of the two painters entering an artistic dialogue, united in time and place.

In contrast to Monet's picture—which has some flat areas—Renoir's has a scintillating all-over dappled facture that engulfs us. Strong diagonals introduce dynamism which are counterbalanced by the verticals of the trees. The equal amount of light and dark areas and the stabilising quality of foreground mid-tones make the picture especially formally satisfying. The sinuous trunks and branches on the left and top edges encroach on the horizontal surfaces, while more static forms to the right and bottom create another type of dynamic contrast.

Renoir, in this instance, was not designing a composition from scratch but copying what he found. It was his comprehension of design that allowed him to notice and crop an existing scene in a way that led to a painting so satisfyingly dense and dramatic.

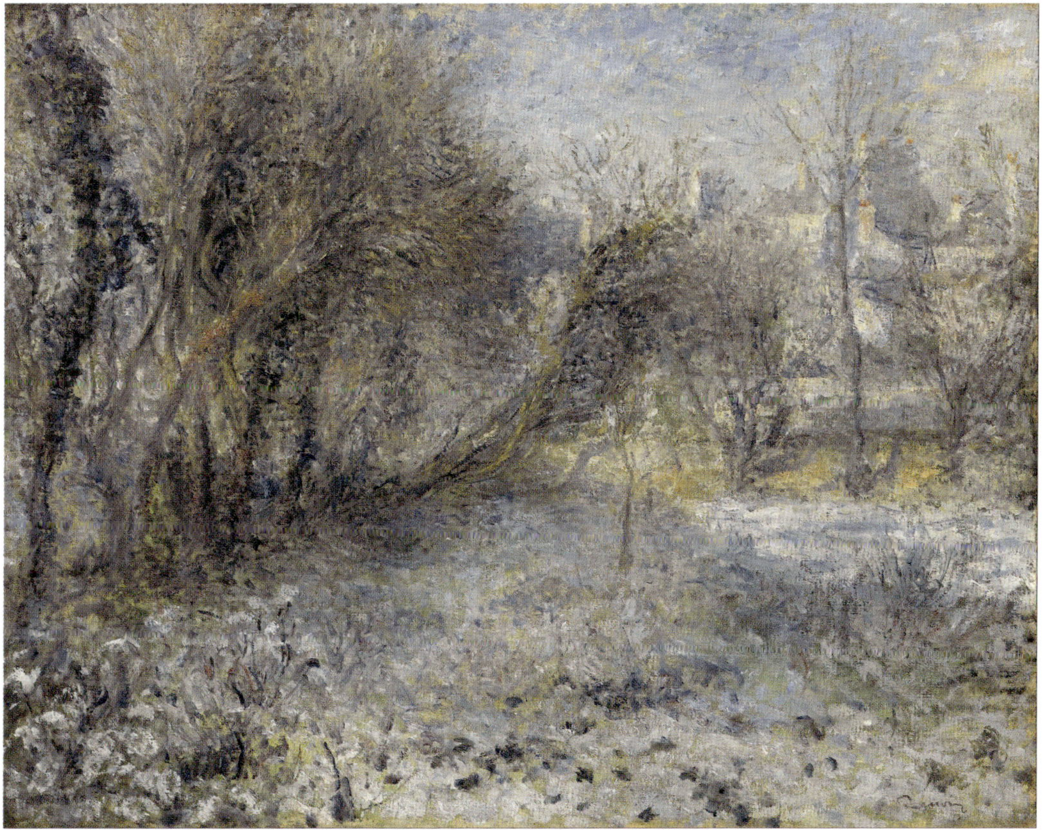

The Skiff (La Yole), 1875

Oil on canvas
71 × 92 cm
The National Gallery, London

The Seine was a centre for leisure activity for Parisians of all classes. Cafés, restaurants and dance halls catered to visitors; some were situated on stationary boats and barges. Punts, skiffs and rowing boats were available for hire; a *yole* is a narrow, lightweight rowing boat. The location of this scene may be Chatou—a regular haunt for the Impressionists and where Renoir is known to have painted—but it may be an amalgam of multiple places.

It was the expansion of the suburban railway and omnibus networks that made the villages on the fringes of Paris available to the middle and working classes. Renoir has included a train in the top right of the painting, partially concealed by trees.

The Impressionists found piquant topics in these riverside settings, which they share with the stories of Guy de Maupassant. Renoir and Maupassant knew each other slightly but did not become close, distanced by their very different temperaments. Renoir found too many of Maupassant's stories sad or morbid.

The use of pure colours, tonally adjusted with the addition of white, gives this painting particular vibrancy. The use of complementary colours in the juxtaposing of the orange boat and blue water heighten both hues. The male figure is given pale linen clothing; the woman's dress is white and tinted with the blue of the water. This demonstrates the Impressionists' interest in recreating the effect of reflected colour, where the proximity of areas of colour produces an admixture, especially on pale-surfaced objects. Renoir (and Degas) particularly applied this observation to the nudes they painted by adding tints of other colours reflecting off the pale skin.

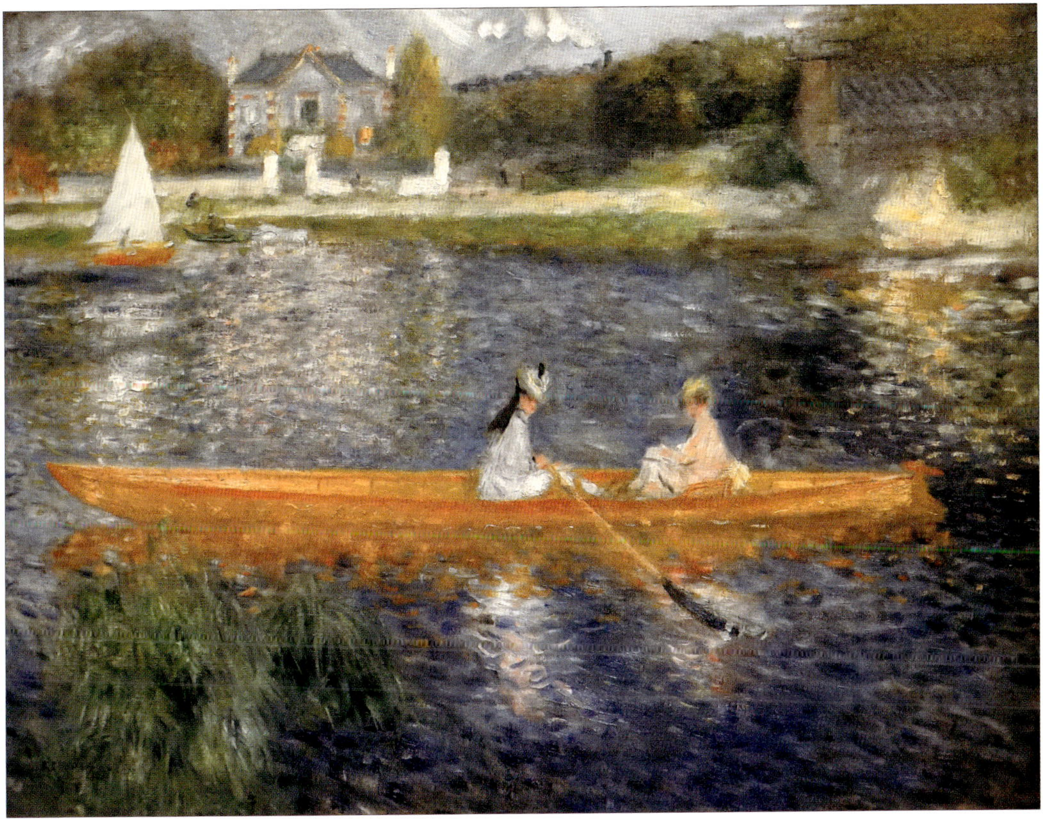

Lunch at the Restaurant Fournaise (The Rowers' Lunch), 1875

Oil on canvas
100.4 × 80.9 cm
The Art Institute of Chicago

On a sunny afternoon a couple of rowers and their female companion take a rest from boating to dine at a riverside restaurant. The blazing day outside reflects from the water and turns the interior into a shimmering box of light and warmth. The haziness of forms and lack of volumetric modelling gives this painting a beguiling, dreamy quality. Situated on the Île de la (Grande) Jatte, an islet on the Seine frequented by the Impressionists and where Seurat would paint *A Sunday on La Grande Jatte* (1884–6), was a restaurant called La Fournaise. Renoir was on friendly terms with the proprietor Alphonse Fournaise, who allowed him and his models to occupy a table so that he could paint this picture and, a few years later, *Luncheon of the Boating Party* (1879–1881) (page 73).

This painting was exhibited in 1876 at the second Independent exhibition. Durand-Ruel bought it and shipped it to his New York branch in 1892, from where it immediately entered a private American collection. It was donated to The Art Institute of Chicago in 1922. Renoir's later financial security derived from American enthusiasm for Impressionism. ("We perhaps owe to the Americans that we did not die of hunger.") Some of his masterpieces had left France by the 1890s. Alfred Barnes's foundation established in Merion, Pennsylvania houses the world's best collection of Renoir, rivalled only by that of the Musée d'Orsay.

A comforting depiction of everyday life in Belle-Époque Paris, *Lunch at the Restaurant Fournaise* is the sort of painting that appeals to many as emblematic of a golden era, but one that troubles some historians, who characterise such depictions as an avoidance of material realities. Among the Impressionists, Pissarro alone engaged in social realism, although social observation and satire was practised by most Impressionists. Renoir outrightly rejected Pissarro's attitude, instead embracing art as a source of sensuous distraction.

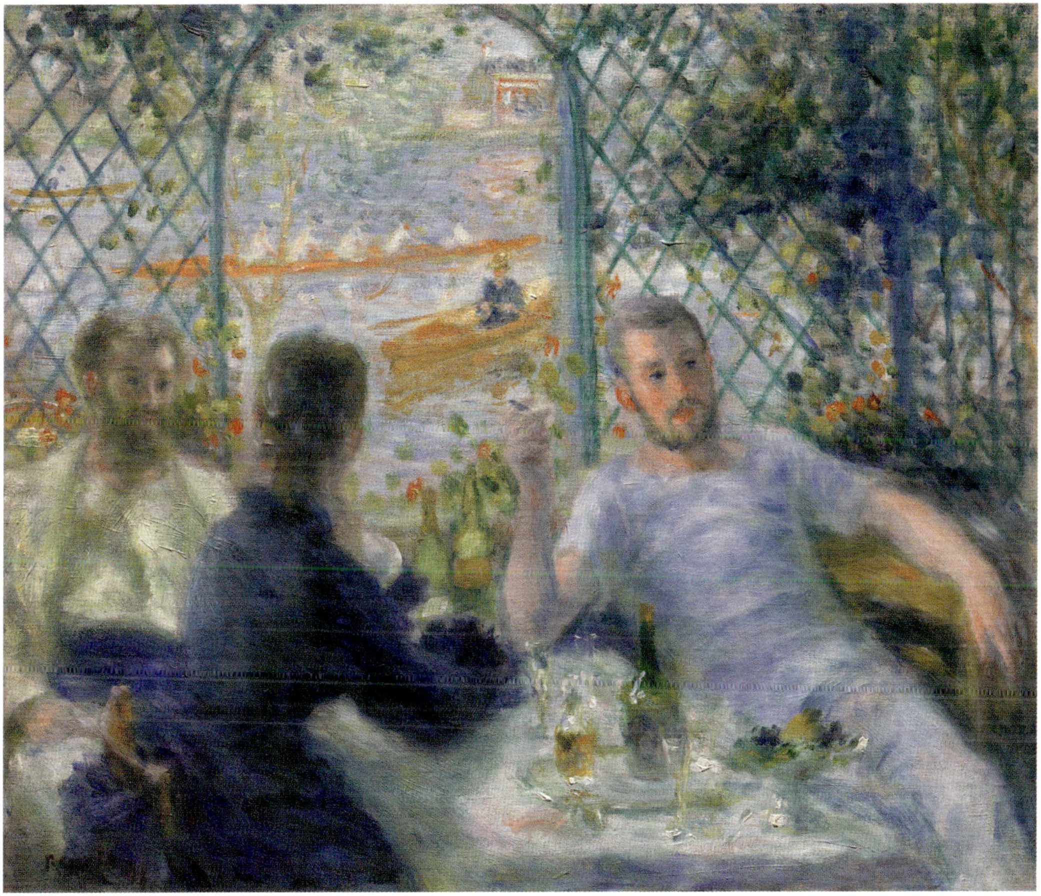

Nude in Sunlight, 1875/6

Oil on canvas
81 × 65 cm
Musée d'Orsay, Paris

This painting of a young woman is as indistinct and soft as the figures in *Lunch at the Restaurant Fournaise* (1875) (page 63). The skin of the model is tinted by reflected light, presented in dappled shade. She is depicted in a moment of stillness, surrounded by a strongly directional description of foliage and drapery that form a vortex of movement around her.

When it was exhibited in the second Independent exhibition in 1876, the critic Albert Wolff denounced this painting. "Try to explain to M. Renoir that the body of a woman is not a mass of decomposing flesh, with the green and purple spots that denote the entire putrefaction of a corpse!" The Impressionists had realised that objects reflected adjacent colours and that pale objects often take on the tints of light. These observations were rejected by conservative artists and critics, who influenced public responses. For them skin was white, cream or pink, never tinted green, blue or orange. Impressionist painting was roundly rejected by many as being grotesque or malicious. The claim that the painters were trying to pass off loose preparatory sketches as finished pictures carried the imputation that the exhibitors were committing fraud and bringing their profession into disrepute. Although the Impressionists trenchantly defended their offerings—an effort sympathetic critics joined them in—the criticism cut deep. Partially in response to these attacks, Renoir made his figures better defined and more solid in his paintings, such as *Two Sisters* (1881) (page 75) and then to a more extreme degree in the Ingresque period.

Accusations of immorality and sedition—political as well as aesthetic—caused Renoir, who was nervous about respectable collectors being scared off, to distance himself from Impressionist exhibitions. He was an adventurous independent creator and an insecure artisan, afflicted by working-class social anxiety and fear of poverty.

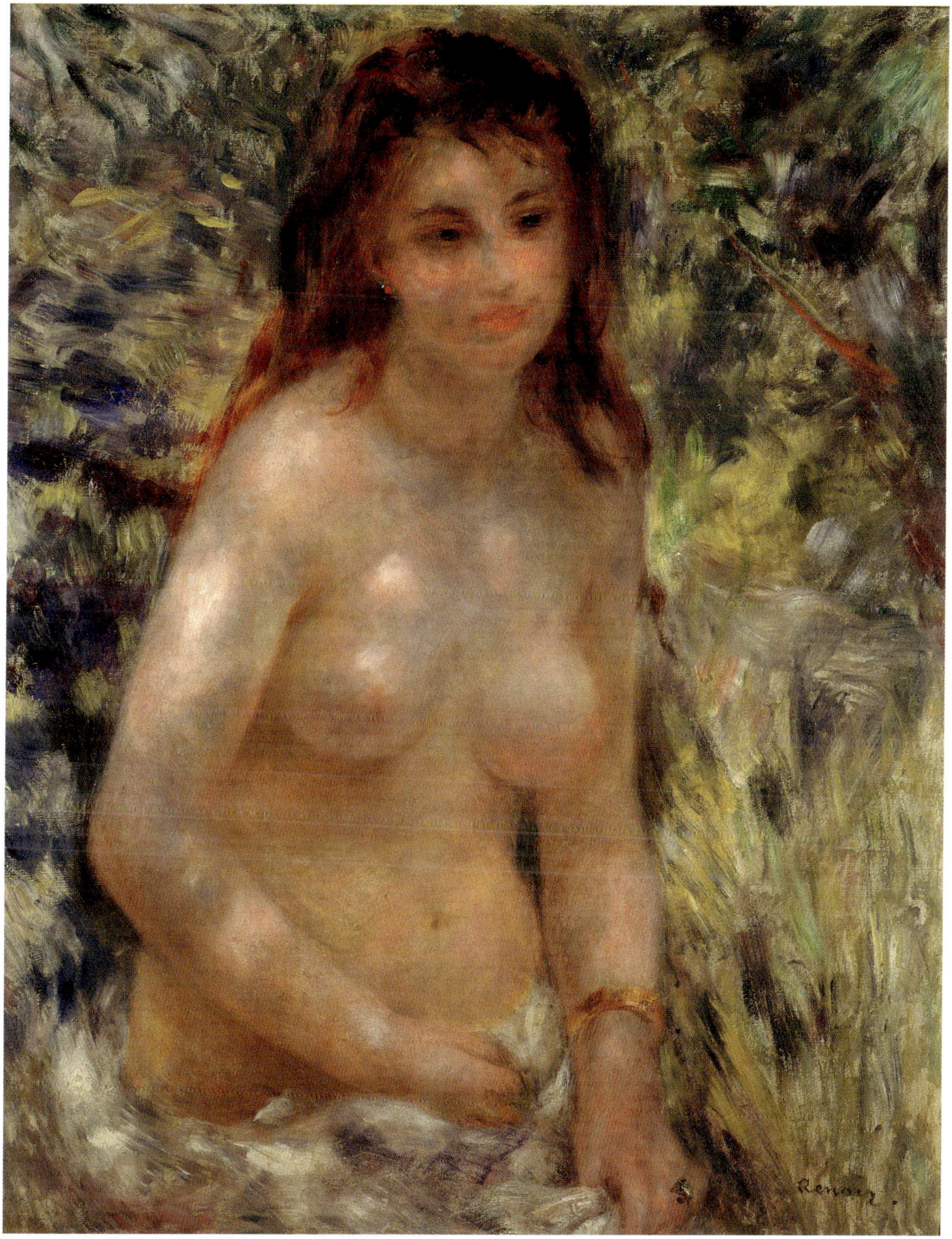

A Girl with Watering Can, 1876

Oil on canvas
100 × 73 cm
Chester Dale Collection, National Gallery of Art, Washington DC

This attractive portrait of a young child is one of Renoir's most popular paintings. Despite wishing to create more ambitious works of art, Renoir made his living in the early years from portraiture. By the time of the first Independent exhibition, he was already deemed the portraitist of the Impressionist group. However, like his friend Degas, Renoir never treated portraiture as mere drudgery. Throughout his career, the artist produced engaged and inventive portraits, meeting the minimum standard, namely pleasing his subjects.

The success of the Charpentier family group portrait (page 17) at the Salon of 1879 brought the painter numerous portrait commissions. Women and children were considered particularly suitable for Renoir's flattering depictions. He had an affinity with children and displayed evident patience with his own. Those who met him stated Renoir was quite reserved and noncommittal, leaving interlocutors with an agreeable impression. This seems to have carried over into his behaviour with children, with acquaintances later remembering the painter as patient and gentle with his young portrait-sitters.

The subject of this painting is unknown, so it may have been painted by Renoir just because he found the appearance of the child prepossessing. The delicacy in the brushwork echoes that found in the contemporaneous portrait of Irene Cahen d'Anvers (page 19).

This painting was bequeathed to the National Gallery of Art by American collector Chester Dale in 1962, who acted as president of the gallery. His remarkable private collection of modern painting from the nineteenth and twentieth centuries has greatly enriched the museum's holdings of great Impressionist painting since their 1963 bequest.

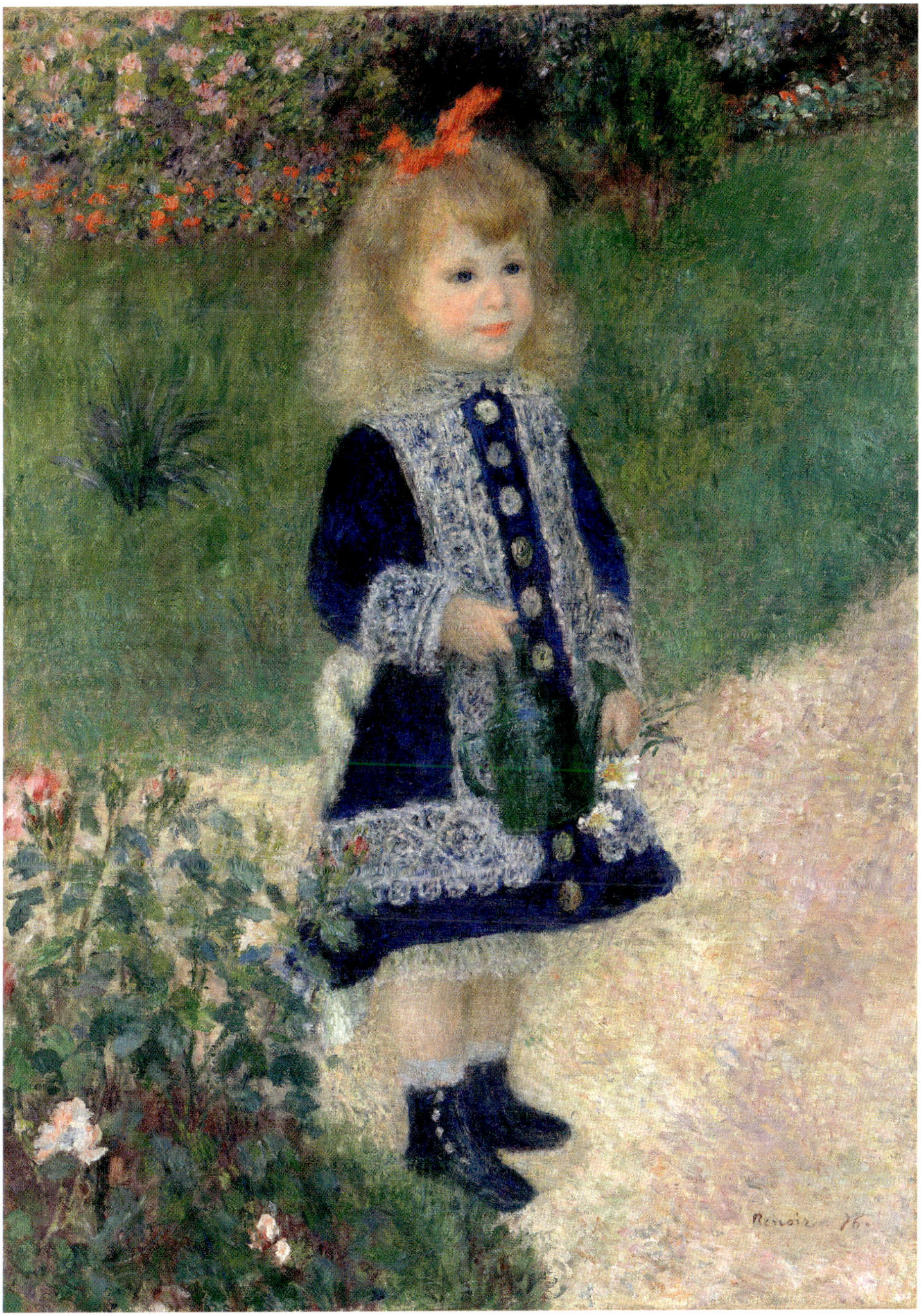

The Ball at Le Moulin de la Galette, 1876

Oil on canvas
131.5 × 176.5 cm
Musée d'Orsay, Paris

The Moulin de la Galette was a popular open-air café with music situated in Montmartre. The institution had grown around a mill (*moulin*) where bakers sold cakes or pancakes called "*galettes*". Exhibited in the Independent exhibition with Impressionists in 1877, Philippe Burty gave this painting great praise. "With a few brushstrokes [Renoir] emphasizes the stationary objects, chairs, benches, tables. He endows the groups of dancers and of talkers with their own truth of action, and renders the rays of sunshine with palpitating brushstrokes."
"This is a historical document, a priceless monument to Parisian life, scrupulously faithful. Nobody before had thought to set down such an everyday event on such a large-scale canvas; his boldness will be rewarded with well-deserved success." Although Rivière's 1877 response to this picture omits the precedent of Courbet, in essence he correctly identifies the replacement of the noble subject with the documentation of ordinary life as Renoir's achievement with his Parisian scenes. The author also neglects to mention that he modelled for one of the figures in the painting. Other models include Lhôte, artists Franc-Lamy, Cordey and Norbert Goeneutte; two of the women are Margot and Estelle, regular models for Renoir.
This painting has become for us the quintessential snapshot of Montmartre's heyday as a site of revelry and leisure, a period, roughly speaking, which lasted from the end of the Commune in 1871 up to 1905. By the latter date, this painting had been hanging in the Musée du Luxembourg, Paris for a decade, donated by Caillebotte. The popularity of this picture—in addition to stories about Montmartre's writers and artists—led to the beginnings of commercialisation in this once disreputable and disparaged district of Paris, previously associated with poverty, anarchism, debauchery and prostitution. By 1900, when Picasso painted his nocturnal *Le Moulin de la Galette*—a tribute to Renoir—Montmartre was not yet a tourist site.

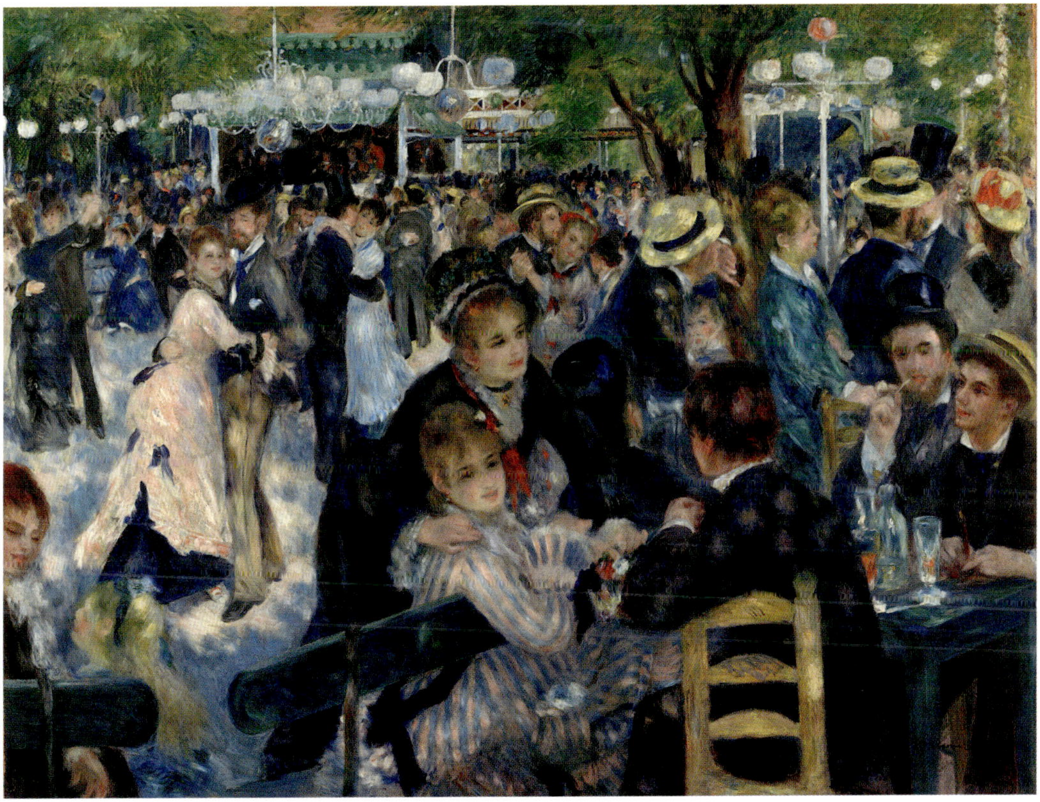

The Swing, 1876

Oil on canvas
92 × 73 cm
Musée d'Orsay, Paris

Renoir was well aware of Fragonard's famous painting *The Swing* (1767), depicting a woman flirting with a man in a verdant glade. Renoir's painting is more sedate and genteel, a modern manifestation of courtship in a public garden in the metropolis. The woman seems detached and contemplative, her companions are attentive, perhaps in the process of flattering her or engaging in casual conversation. A young girl watches the adult interaction, imperfectly gleaning something of her future as a woman. Jean Renoir identified the location for this painting as being "the restaurant at the top of rue des Saules" in Montmartre. This picture, made the same year as *Le Moulin de la Galette*, acts as a counterpoint to that hectic, bawdy scene. The settings of the two tableaux are very close, as this garden probably belonged to the Moulin de la Galette. Renoir hired a cheap lodging in Montmartre so that he could spend as much time as possible working on his Moulin de la Galette paintings in situ.
The woman is the actress Jeanne Samary, whom Renoir would depict in individual portraits as well as group scenes; the men are Goeneutte and Edmond Renoir. The artist painted actresses and singers many times, as they were used to being scrutinised. Their celebrity boosted the portraitist's credibility in the eyes of potential patrons. Following inclusion in the third Independent exhibition, *The Swing* was purchased by Gustave Caillebotte. Caillebotte was an artist and painter, who exhibited in Independent exhibitions. He trusted Renoir as a friend and appointed him executor of his will. Upon Caillebotte's death in 1894 a bequest was made of his collection to the Louvre. At that time state officials were opposed to accepting a large donation of Impressionist art, considering it not sufficiently august for the world's greatest art museum. Only after considerable negotiation—in which Renoir played a part—did the Louvre accept half of the donation, later transferred to the Musée du Luxembourg, then to the Musée d'Orsay.

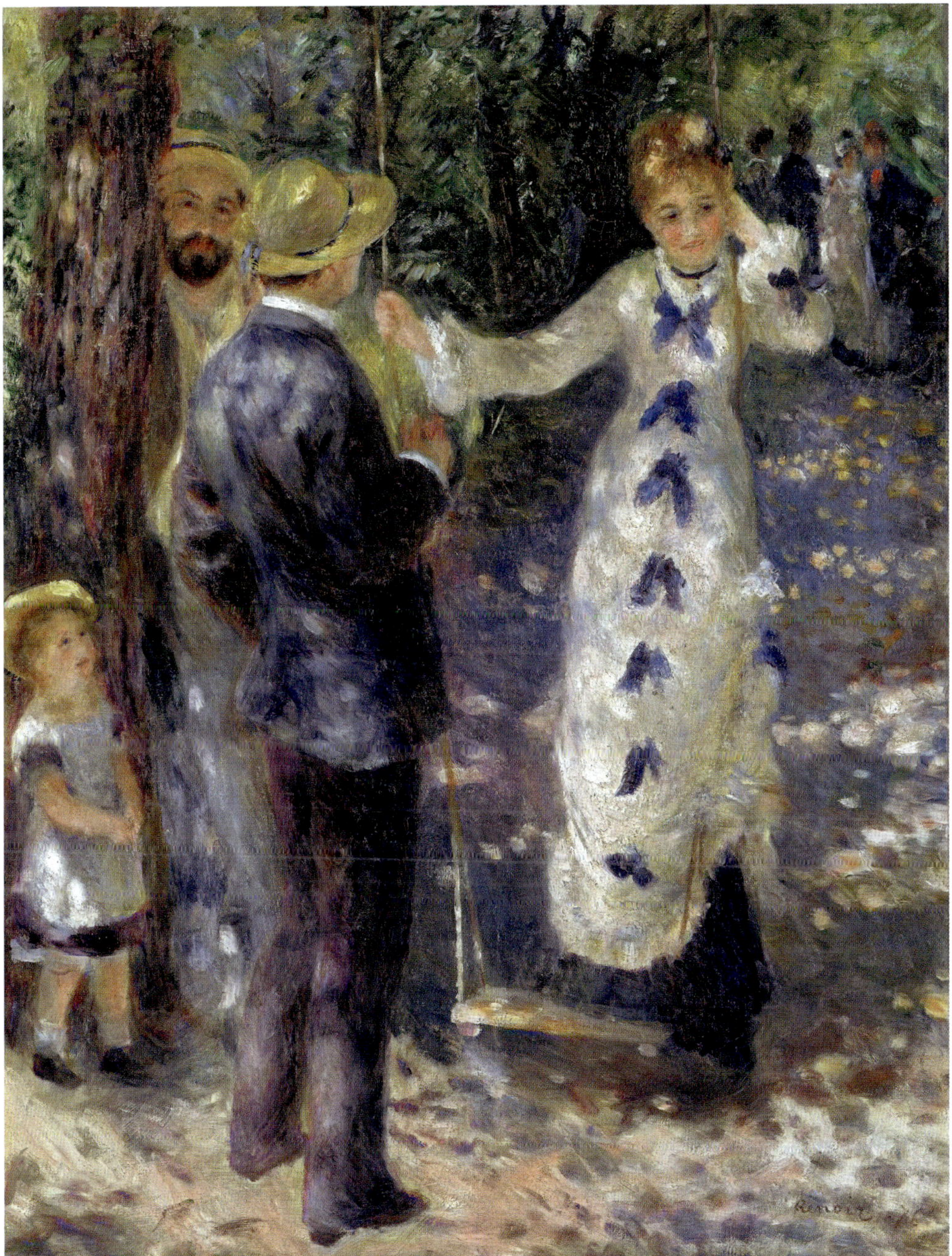

Luncheon of the Boating Party, 1880/1

Oil on canvas
130.2 × 175.6 cm
Philips Collection, Washington DC

Renoir was aware that this painting was particularly ambitious. He wrote in 1881, "I am doing a picture of a boating party that I have been itching to do for a long time .... It's a good thing from time to time to attempt something beyond one's powers".
On a summer afternoon at La Fournaise, a group of boaters mix with city girls and well-dressed Parisian men. All are engaged in the process of conversation or flirting, seemingly having finished their meal. The large cast of animated characters and the capturing of the atmosphere of a balmy convivial setting have cemented this picture as the apotheosis of French romance. Many have been impressed by the acuity of Renoir's presentation of personal and inter-class dynamics.
At the bottom left Aline plays with a dog; other models are Baron Raoul Barbier, collector Charles Ephrussi and his secretary, poet Jules Laforgue, actresses Ellen Andrée, Jeanne Samary and Angèle, two children of the restaurant proprietor (Alphonse Fournaise Junior and Alphonsine Fournaise), journalist M. Maggiolo, Lhôte, Lestringuez and Caillebotte. Although its commencement date has been put at 1876—to coincide with *Lunch at the Restaurant Fournaise* (page 63)—research suggests this canvas was started in 1879 or 1880. We know it was finished shortly before Durand-Ruel purchased it in the summer of 1881. It was that payment that enabled Renoir to travel to Italy.
Unfortunately, relining—affixing the painted surface to a fresh backing support—and cleaning has altered the appearance. The awning stripes are less clear than they were, forms have become flatter and the stripping of some of Renoir's delicate glazes has removed some of the rich colouring of the painting. Renoir's oil paintings are especially vulnerable to incautious cleaning with solvents. He never varnished his own pictures, understanding that clear varnish can alter the appearance and tonal values of a picture. Removal of discoloured protective clear top-level varnish can easily include irreparable removal of the artist's tinted glazes just below that upper surface.

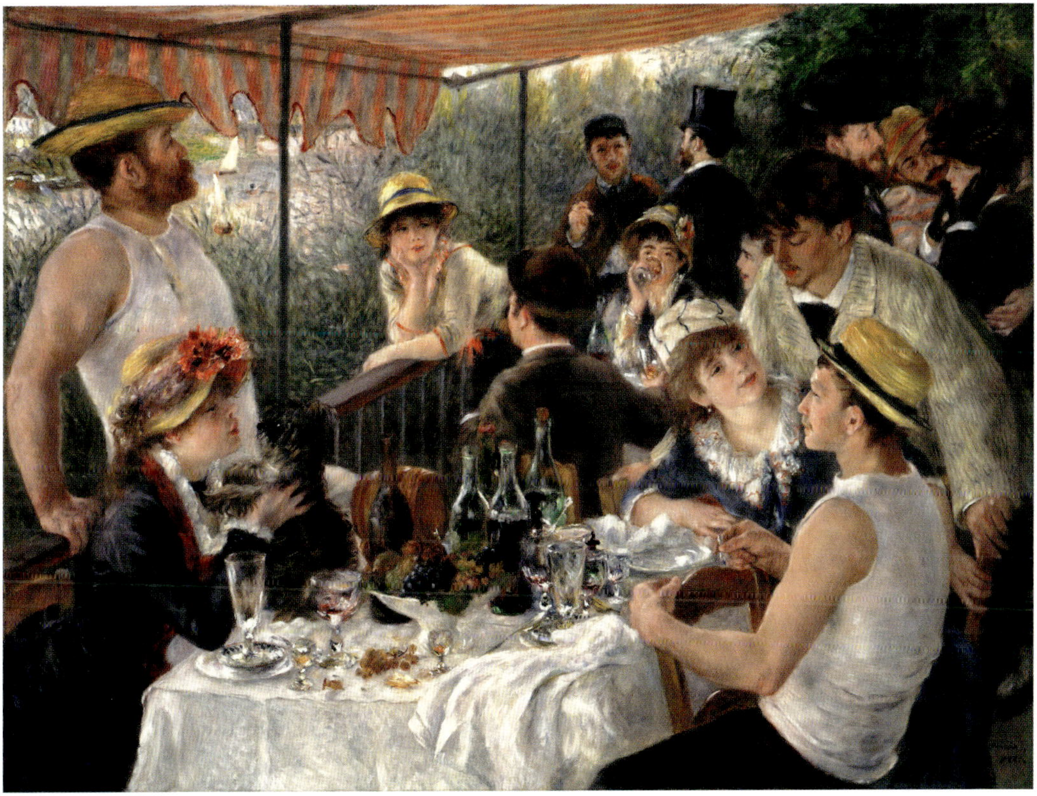

Two Sisters (On the Terrace), 1881

Oil on canvas
100.4 × 80.9 cm
The Art Institute of Chicago

This painting—which we should perhaps call a double portrait—features an attractive young woman and a young girl, subjects of which Renoir had already proved his mastery. Originally called "Woman on a Terrace beside the Seine", the setting of this painting is the terrace of the La Fournaise restaurant on the Isle of Grande Jatte. Apparently, the figures are not actually sisters. The figure on the left is Jeanne Darlot, who was about 18 years old at the time, and would later become an actress; no firm identification of the child has been established.

The most prominent areas of red are on the hats of the figures, drawing attention to the faces and emphasising the double presence. By such means, Renoir indicates that this is a double portrait rather than a portrait of a young woman with a child. The reds stand out because of the predominantly blue-and-green surroundings and the deep blue of the figures' outfits. Earth hues were kept to a minimum, as was common among Impressionists. Hence the colour of the barrel being changed to blue from its natural muted brown or grey; this means it also does not detract from the areas of pure red. Renoir would comment to associates that his paintings would look best after half a century, once the strongest colours had faded a little, making the palette less strident. At this time, it seems that Renoir, apparently irked by criticism that his motifs had little definition, was attempting to make his figures more solid. The background and surroundings are softer than ever, indicative of Renoir moving towards the Ingresque period, when backgrounds would become more insubstantial and figures more sharply defined. Such division between soft and crisp in single pictures demonstrated to sceptics that Renoir had full command of such distinctions, thereby establishing his competence.

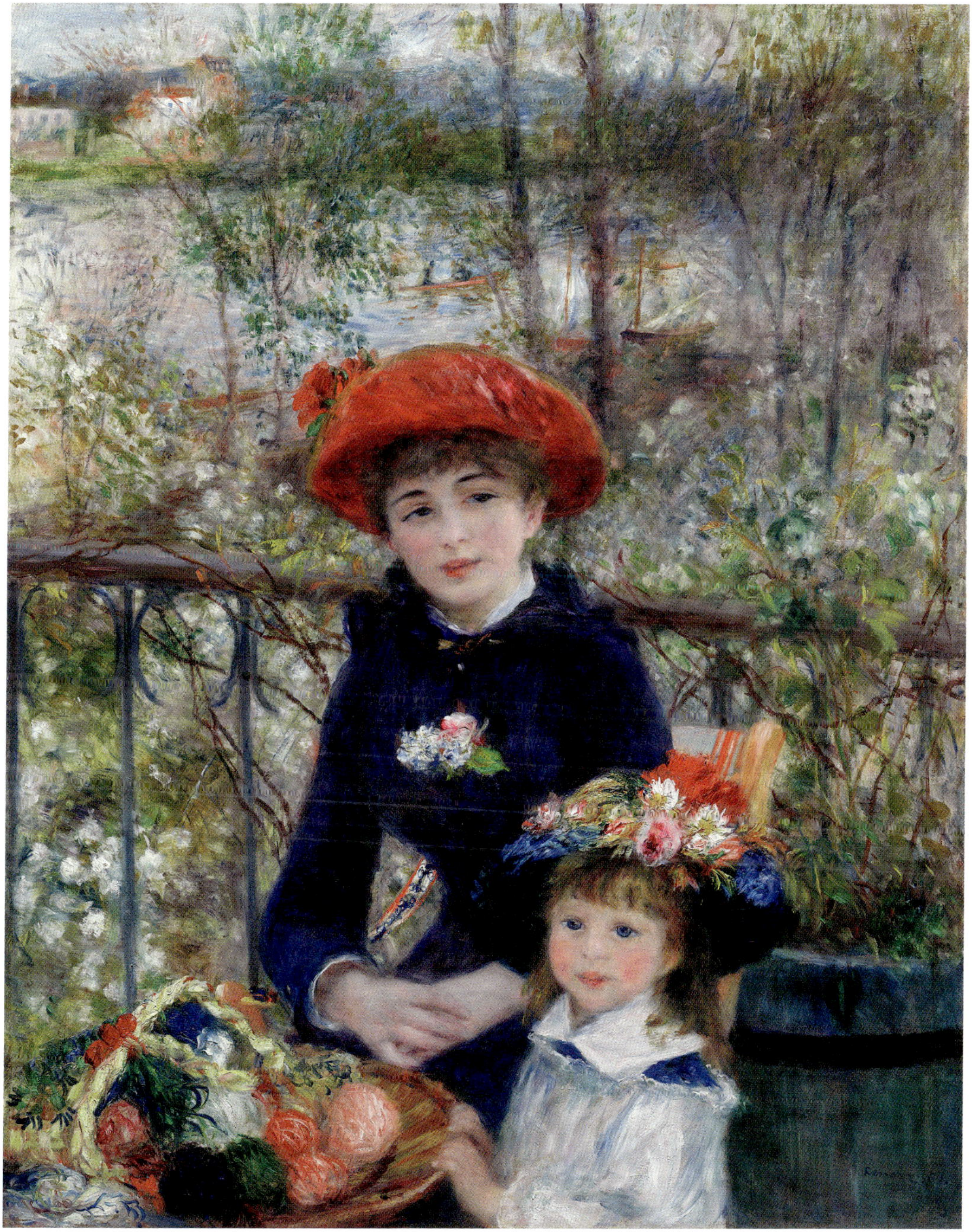

The Umbrellas, c. 1881–6

Oil on canvas
180.3 × 114.9 cm
The National Gallery, London

Pedestrians intersect in a rainy Parisian street. We can detect a touch of Cézanne in the tumble of curving facets of the titular umbrellas. Unlike other Impressionists, who used figures sparingly in street scenes, Renoir has almost filled the entire surface with figures and umbrellas—similar to his *Le Moulin de la Galette* (page 69).

This painting was completed in two stages. Historians have analysed the fashions and discovered that they are separated by about five years, which examination of Renoir's technique also confirms. The right side of the painting, including the little girl, was completed in Renoir's Impressionist period. X-radiography reveals it was only roughly sketched in before Renoir commenced painting. The left side—with Valadon modelling for the most prominent figure—was executed in Renoir's later Ingresque classical style and was tightly drawn out beforehand. Once noticed, the disjuncture between the two parts is unignorable, yet the strength of the composition holds together this fractured picture. The unusual genesis of this painting is also apparent in the change of pigments; the right side uses chrome yellow and cobalt blue, the left side Naples yellow and French ultramarine.

Why did Renoir fail to finish the painting during the first phase of its creation? One suspects that it was because he had not solved how to describe rain, wetness and reflections (particularly on the paving)—something that other Impressionists had mastered. In contrast, Renoir did not have an aptitude for portraying wet surfaces. *The Umbrellas* was a studio production, clearly not painted in situ, and Renoir may have abandoned it as unpersuasive. Nonetheless, he must have thought there was enough there to make the painting worthy of completion, after being initially stymied by the picture's problems. Interestingly, this painting is a relative success and has achieved acclaim in spite of its disjointed development.

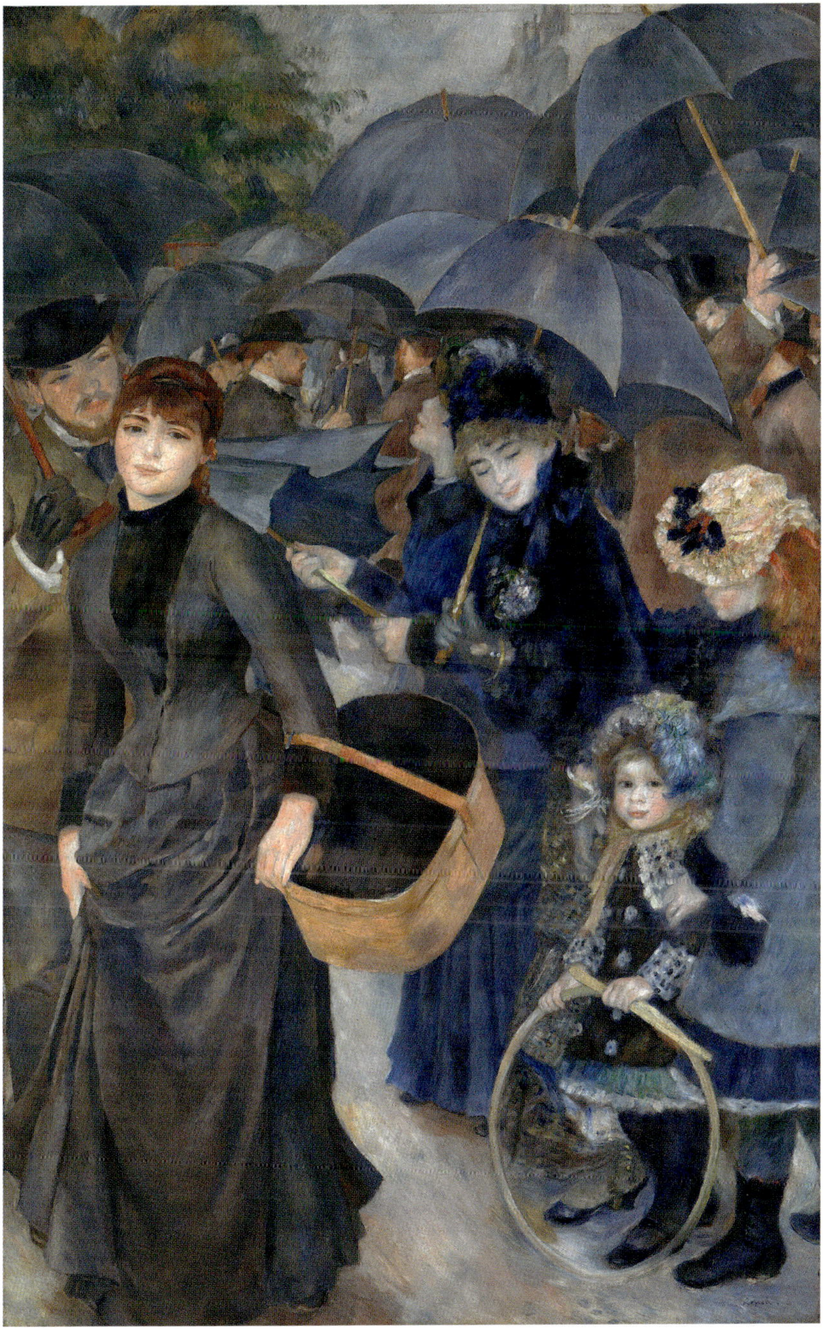

Algerian landscape, 1881

Oil on canvas
65 × 81.5 cm
Musée d'Orsay, Paris

This painting, which has much in common with the handsome canvas *Hills around the Bay of Moulin Huet, Guernsey* (1883) (page 22), depicts a steep uncultivated valley near Algiers. The dabbing of strong colours, modulated with white, builds an undulating terrain and the painting does not contain a single straight line. It shows no sign of any human intervention in nature. For a man of central France, Renoir associates the aloe veras in the foreground with an exotic clime—the blues of the aloe leaves add the only cool hues to the painting, heightening the hot airless quality of the scene. The aloes perform the additional function as a *repousser*, which is a dark area placed in the lower foreground close to the viewer separating him/her from the scene and serving to deepen pictorial space.
Renoir arrived in Algeria on 4 March 1881 and stayed about one month in what was then considered a *departement* of France. During his time there he stayed in Mustapha, a suburb of the city of Algiers. He commented on the fecundity of the landscape and mentioned in a letter that he was planning to visit the desert. That fecundity is particularly apparent in this painting and a contemporaneous one of a banana plantation. In that painting, he was excited by the striking serrated arcs of the banana leaves, which formed a thick band running across the centre of the scene. His other subjects were mosques and a park. He made a second visit to Algiers from early March to late April 1882, during which he painted genre subjects and portraits.
This painting dates from his first stay. There is no explanation for the subtitle "The Ravine of the Wild Woman", which is not a term that was used for any place near Algiers.

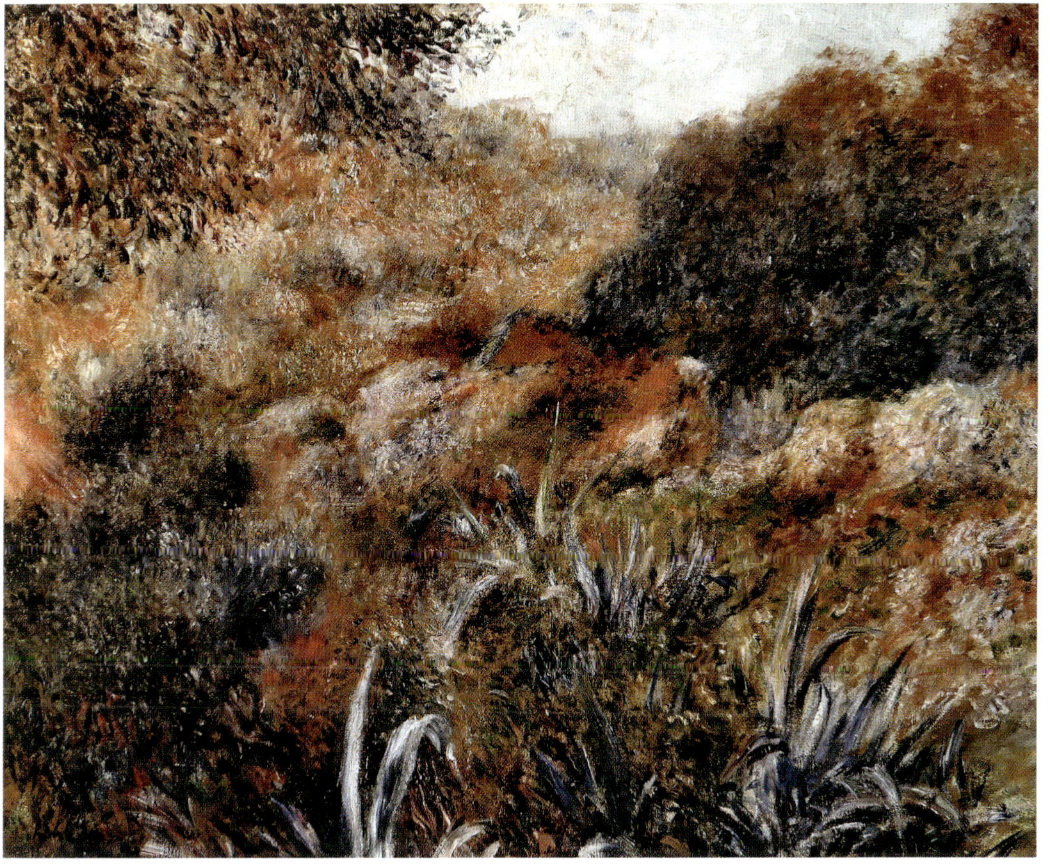

The Piazza San Marco, Venice, 1881

Oil on canvas
89.5 × 104.5 cm
The John R. Van Derlip Fund, Minneapolis Institute of Arts, Minnesota

The existing Byzantine-Gothic-style Basilica of Saint Mark is the third building to be named as such on that site in Venice and was erected in the eleventh century. The basilica and the square it overlooks are considered the heart of Venice.
This scene has been painted by Gentile Bellini, Canaletto, Turner, Whistler and many other prominent artists. Renoir noted that when he made this view (in autumn 1881) he was surrounded by other artists painting the same scene as him, one that has become close to cliché.
At the time Renoir was in Venice, there had been vigorous efforts—headed by British art critic John Ruskin—to prevent the modernisation of the basilica; these attempts largely succeeded, although some mosaics had already been replaced before authorities decided to preserve the building in toto.
Renoir praised the Roman murals he saw in Pompeii and the Naples museum, and the frescoes of Raphael in Rome. In contrast, it seems the paintings of Giorgione, Titian, Tintoretto and Veronese made less impression on him during his sojourn to Venice. This seems most likely because Renoir was already very familiar with good examples of their art to be found in the Louvre. It may also be because he was considering how he might develop his own painting in a tighter, less painterly style, that was more classical in character. When he saw it in person, Renoir admired the Basilica of San Marco. "Symmetrical, as a whole, but not one detail is like another!"
Liberated by the Impressionist credo of fast and direct painting *en plein air*, Renoir has brought fresh life to a motif that had—even by the 1880s—become stale. Colour is riotous, with lightened sienna or ochre used for masonry; deep blue and vermilion describe shadows. The zooming piazza paving directs our eye to the second rightmost alcove, introducing a tension between that point and the main doorway—the darkest point in the painting and centre of the building. Visible in the bottom corners is the white-lead primer that Renoir used to prepare his canvases. This prefigures the energetic Fauvist approach that relied on strong mark-making and partially visible support surfaces.

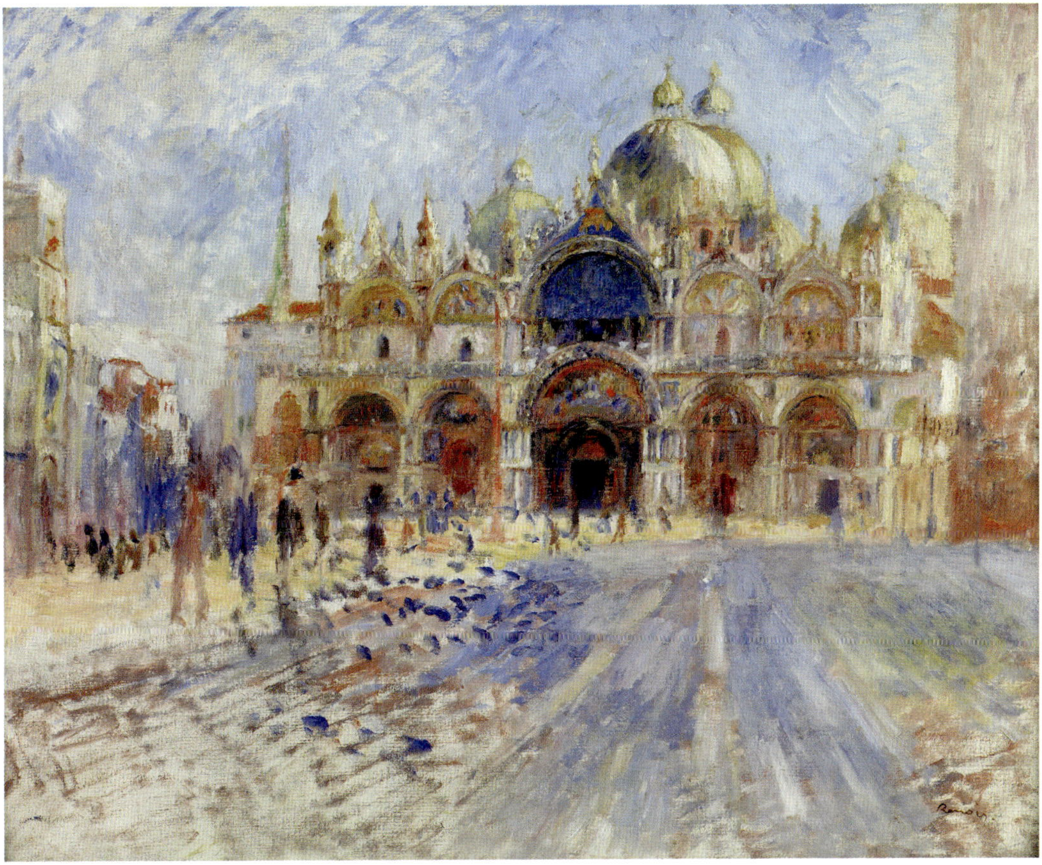

Blonde Bather I, 1881

Oil on canvas
81.6 × 65.4 cm
Clarke Art Institute, Williamstown, Massachusetts

This painting was submitted to the Salon and refused. Aline modelled for the artist, apparently in the open air at Capri. In a second, more artificial version of this painting, Renoir refined his approach on the threshold of his Classical period, using deeper blue to accentuate the pallor of the woman. The Romantic approach found in the sweetness of the face and the dramatic, invented landscape shows Renoir consciously separating himself from the Impressionist tenet of depicting the real world first hand.
This painting is a turning point, where Renoir chooses as his central subject the nude figure—one associated with classical (not Impressionist) art. It was a choice made in response to his experience in Italy. "I have seen the Raphaels in Rome. They are very beautiful and I should have seen them before. They are full of knowledge and wisdom. He did not try to do impossible things, like me. But they're beautiful. I prefer Ingres for oil painting. But the frescoes, they are admirable in their simplicity and nobility."
In particular, this painting echoes the Venuses created by the Old Masters. Landscape and still-life were ideal subjects for Impressionists wishing to experiment with broken colour, light and weather effects and the juxtaposition of patterns and colour. For such reasons, landscape was seen as an ideal forum for advanced painting in France during the middle decades of the nineteenth century, specifically because it did not have an academic pedigree. The Impressionists, wanting to address issues of colour, light and perception, preferred paintings viewers could not "read" quickly like a book—as one can with an anecdotal vignette—or automatically recognise as a response to the Old Masters. The nude carried a lot of weight, as it was a subject of art from antiquity onwards and was a grand theme in a way the less-established and less-esteemed genres of the still-life, flower painting and landscape were not. By choosing the nude, Renoir was diverging from this anti-historical approach of the Impressionists. Among the Impressionists, only Degas (who in fact preferred to think of himself as a Realist) and Renoir made significant forays into the nude as a subject.

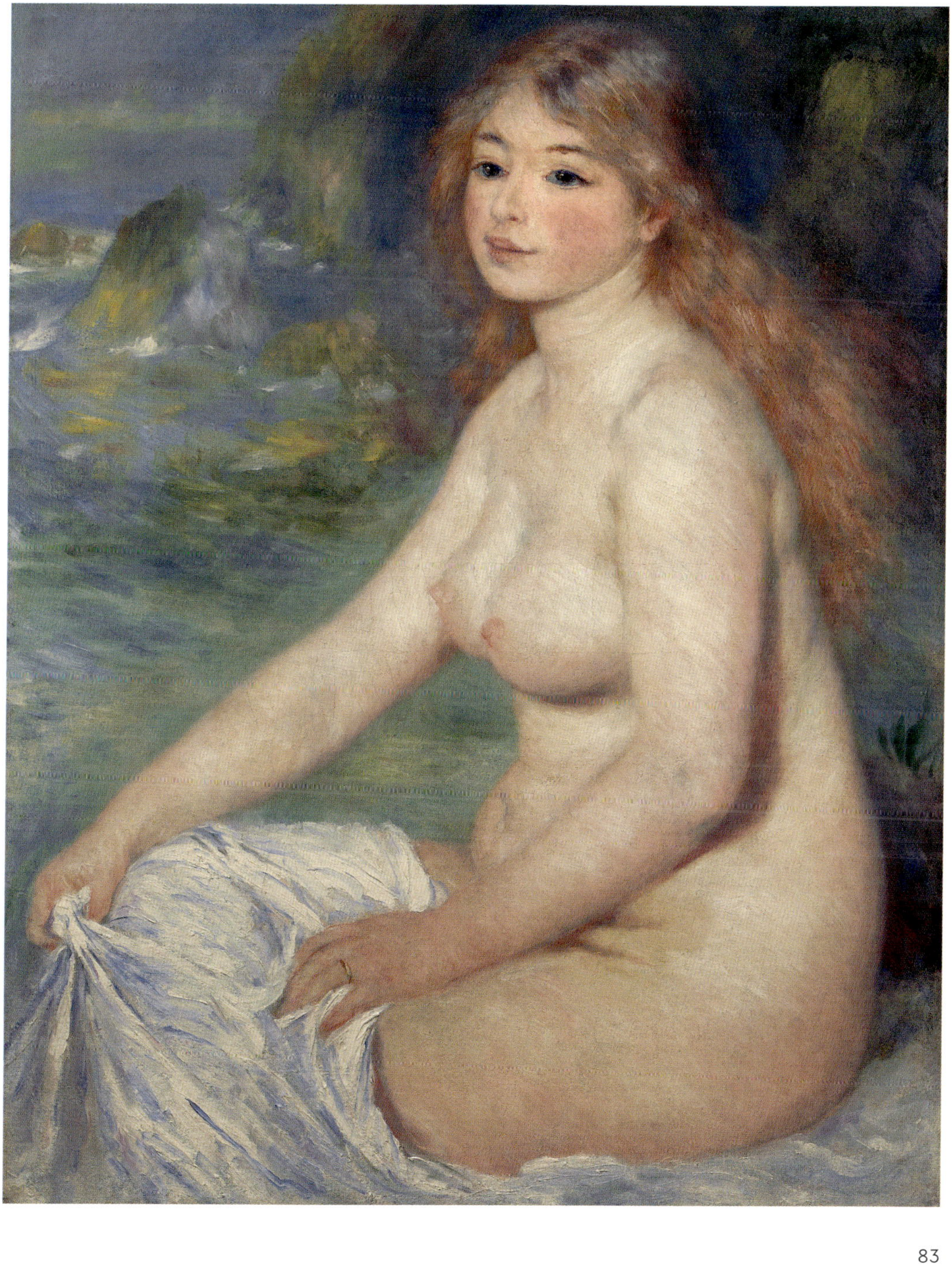

Fruits of the Midi, 1881

Oil on canvas
51 × 65 cm
The Art Institute of Chicago

On a table, a plate overflows with the abundance of a warm and fertile environment. We can recognise aubergine, lemon, pomegranate, pepper and tomato. The painting evidences Renoir's delight in placing strong colours together and depicting different textures. This gathering of fruits typical to the region acts as a portrait in miniature of the hot climate of the Mediterranean coast. The richness of the colour of this painting would produce an echo in the fruit still-lifes by the Nabi painter Félix Vallotton, who was part of the following generation of artists who would find Renoir inspirational.
Boucher, one of Renoir's pantheon of greats, was forever painting peasants revelling in environments replete with fruit. Renoir, never a gourmand or a glutton, had a full appreciation of bountiful food due to his own limiting experience during much of his early life. We have letters in which he wrote about his hunger to colleagues, who also suffered deprivation. Taking an approach contrary to that of Millet and Van Gogh, Renoir declined to depict poverty or the hunger of the poor.
This painting may have been made while Renoir was in Marseilles and l'Estaque, working alongside Cézanne, painting landscapes. It was Cézanne and his future wife Hortense who nursed Renoir after he caught pneumonia. The doctors treating the artist recommended the hot dry climate of North Africa to recover, prompting a second visit to Algiers. Renoir got on well with Cézanne, whose gruff, taciturn character put many people off. He respected Cézanne's early paintings, which some considered uncouth because of their stark tonal contrast and simple forms. Pissarro wrote, "As Renoir said so well, [Cézanne's] paintings have an indefinable quality, like the things of Pompeii, so crude and so admirable". Renoir recognised the power found in Cézanne's early painting is something that fine-art training generally suppresses among professional artists. It may be that he especially admired the forcefulness in Cézanne's art because it was a quality his own art sometimes lacked.

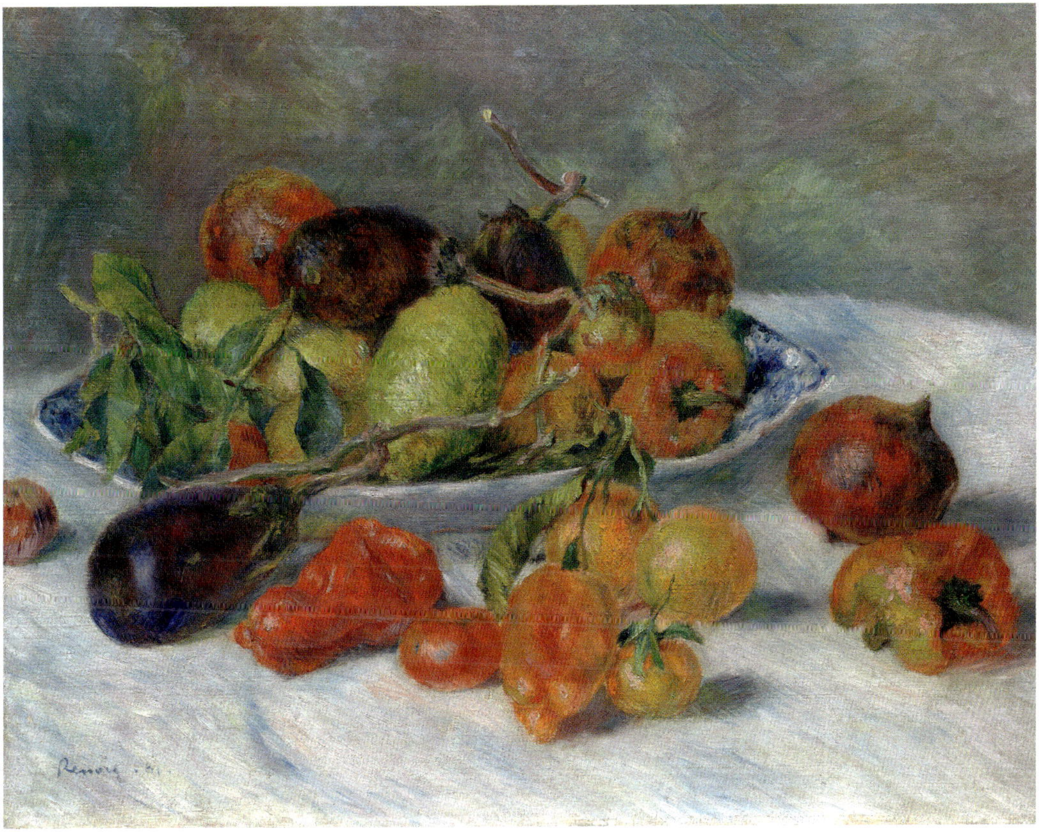

Dance at Bougival, 1883

Oil on canvas
181.9 × 98.1 cm
Museum of Fine Arts, Boston

One of Renoir's most beloved depictions of carefree romance, this painting is part of a trio of canvases of similar proportions but different sizes, depicting dancing couples. Despite Renoir never claiming them to be one, the three pictures have been viewed as an informal triptych. One proposed layout is *Dance at Bougival* on the left, with the rightmost picture being *Dance in the Country* (1883), set in a classier establishment, with a raised dance floor and a balustrade and teacups instead of beer glasses. The male dancer wears no hat and has black shoes instead of shoes of rustic tan leather; the lady has gloves and a more elaborate dress. A straw hat has fallen to the floor; the lady's bonnet is the same as in the Bougival painting. In the centre could have been *Dance in the City* (1883), where an upper-class couple, in evening wear and white gloves, dance in an elegant ballroom with polished stone floor and potted plants by the wall.

In all three paintings, the female dancer is more prominent. Not only do her bright dresses catch the eye more, but her face is also more visible than the man's. Part of the charm of these paintings—and why they remain lodged in our memory—is because they embody the ideal of romantic love by placing the woman at the centre. The woman is romanced, delighted and revered; her pleasure is more important, and her experience is at the core. In each painting, Renoir's sophisticated compositions make the woman the emotional and narrative heart of this expansive depiction of courtship, in three different social worlds.

It is believed Suzanne Valadon modelled in this painting and *Dance in the City*, with Aline appearing in *Dance in the Country*. The male dancer in this painting may be Lhôte, a friend of Renoir.

Settings become progressively higher in class as one considers the set, left to right. *Dance at Bougival* depicts a working-class couple dancing outside an inn in the small rural village of Bougival. Notice that they dance on bare earth, among discarded cigarettes and burnt matches. The diners or drinkers are seated at rough tables on chairs with rush-mat seats. Among the poor people are interlopers from the city, wearing suits and top hats, who took a 20-minute train journey from Gare St-Lazare. The Impressionists were such outsiders themselves, coming to Bougival to paint and relax, falling somewhere between the well-dressed Parisians and the earthy locals. Class distinctions were very obvious to the first viewers of Impressionist pictures and some of the critics' hostility towards the Impressionists derived from implicit recognition that the scenes depict liminal spaces where different classes socialise in a potentially inappropriate or destabilising manner.

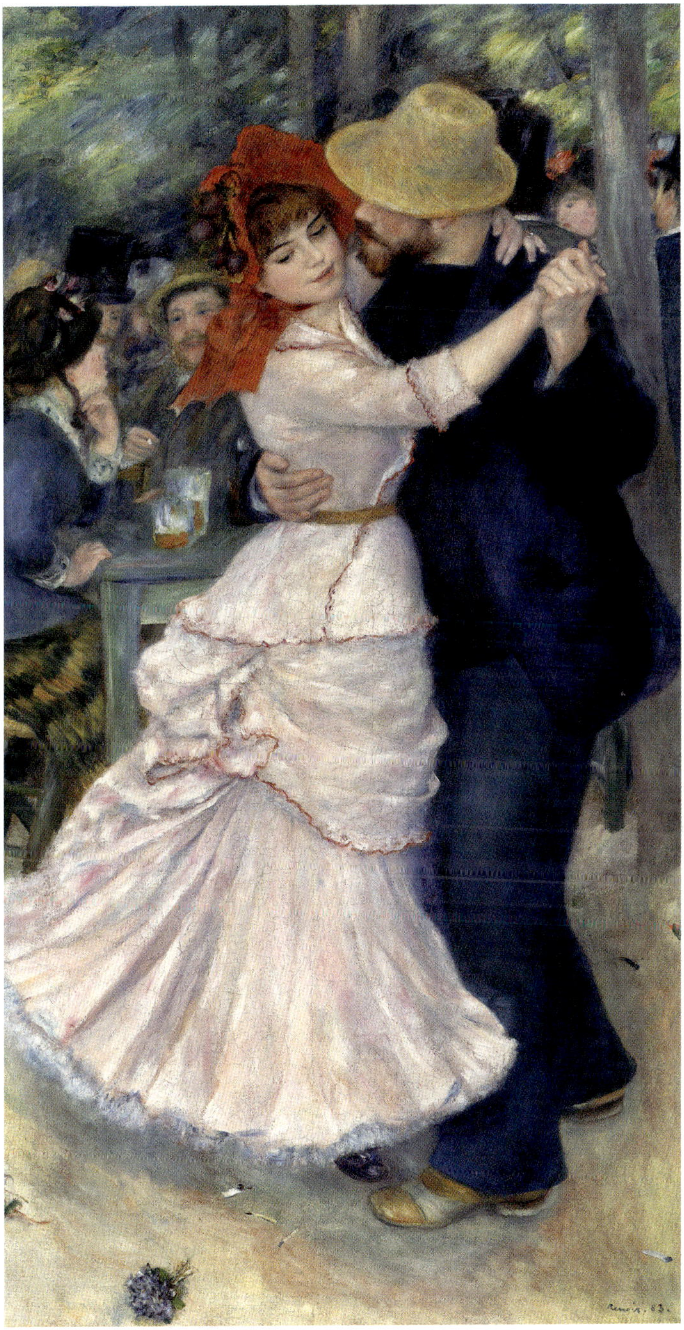

Mediterranean Landscape, c. 1883–91

Oil on canvas
54 × 65.4 cm
Neue Pinakothek Bayerische Staatsgemäldesammlungen, Munich

This is one of Renoir's most audacious landscapes. Reducing sky to a spattering of slivers at the top of the picture, the painter has filled this picture with a deep-shaded hollow through which a path heads, framed by diverse vegetation. The variety of marks indicates the profusion of different plants. Renoir's touch is lively and multi-directional. Notice the tawny-cream dashes indicating dry foliage of high summer, offsetting intense greens flanking the path. The swathe of deep shadow creates a "hole" in the exact centre of the picture, a device that acts as a hook for our attention.
This is an intensely tactile and spatial painting, its depiction of depth masterfully handled. Renoir directs our eye into the centre of a deep space and gives a persuasive sensation of a tunnel leading into a thicket of vigorous vegetation. We sense the way the bough of the old tree on the right stretches out over the path, with an offshoot pushing directly towards us. We imagine that we could construct a rough plan of how the elements are laid out in the terrain, even though there is little detail.
Like the *Snow-covered Landscape* (page 59), this painting gives the impression of having been made on the spot and its relatively small size means it was sufficiently portable for that to be the case. Renoir is not often considered among the masters of the landscape, and it must be admitted that he concentrated mainly on figure paintings. However, on the evidence of the early landscapes selected for this book, a case can be put for Renoir as a truly great landscapist.
No one has been able to establish the location of this unsigned painting, so the designation "Mediterranean" is inexact and estimated. Various dates between 1883 and 1891 have been proposed for its execution, with the Pinakothek curators suggesting c. 1888. However, the technique is closer to Renoir's Impressionist period and therefore I concur with Bailey and Riopelle in their dating of about 1883. I do not see any reason why it might not have been even earlier than that.

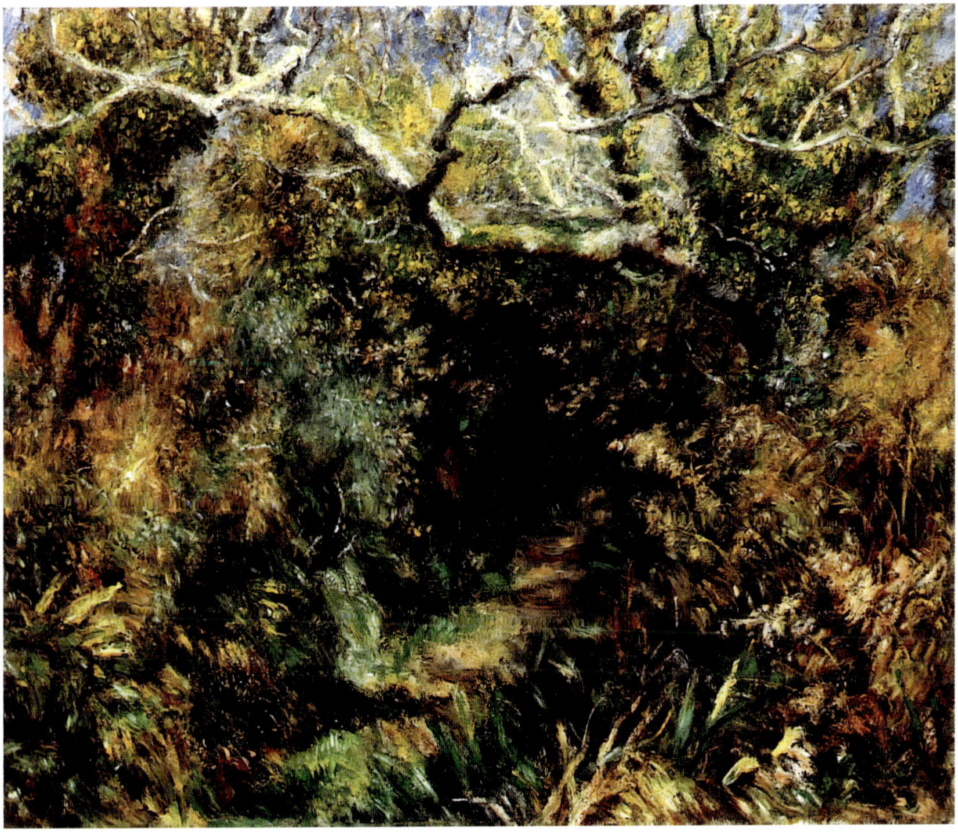

Seated Bather, c. 1883/4

Oil on canvas
119.7 × 93 cm
Fogg Museum, Harvard University

Based on a rough oil sketch (*Bather (Naiad)* (1881)), this carefully painted scene is one of Renoir's most tender treatments of the unclothed figure. The grace and beauty of the woman, based on Aline, are exemplified in the delicate and precisely rendered facial features and fineness of the fingers.

Like *Blonde Bather I* (page 83) and *Blonde Bather II* (1882), the seated woman is presented in a coastal setting. The Salon frequently exposed pictures of semi-nude and nude nymphs and water goddesses, allowing painters to engage with the ostensible subject of mythology with varying degrees of seriousness and discretion. As with harem scenes, these were chances to present female nudes in settings that allowed viewers to indulge in erotic fantasies. Manet's *Luncheon in the Grass* (1863) and *Olympia* (1865) shattered such distancing conventions by situating unclothed figures in contemporary settings. Renoir's female nudes (he painted only one male nude) exist in a nebulous zone—without mythological justification and also lacking disruptive signs of everyday life. Later, in the Rose period, Renoir's nudes are tributes—albeit indirect ones—to the great art of the ancients, the Renaissance and Rococo eras. "I like painting best when it looks eternal without boasting about it: an everyday eternity, revealed on the street corner."

Renoir struggled greatly during his Ingresque classical period. Numerous reports mention him consumed by anxiety and destroying much of his output, dissatisfied with the results of his efforts. Just as the public was becoming more attuned to Impressionism, Renoir had apparently rejected the style. However, following the criticism by fellow artists, dealers and collectors, Renoir would soften his approach.

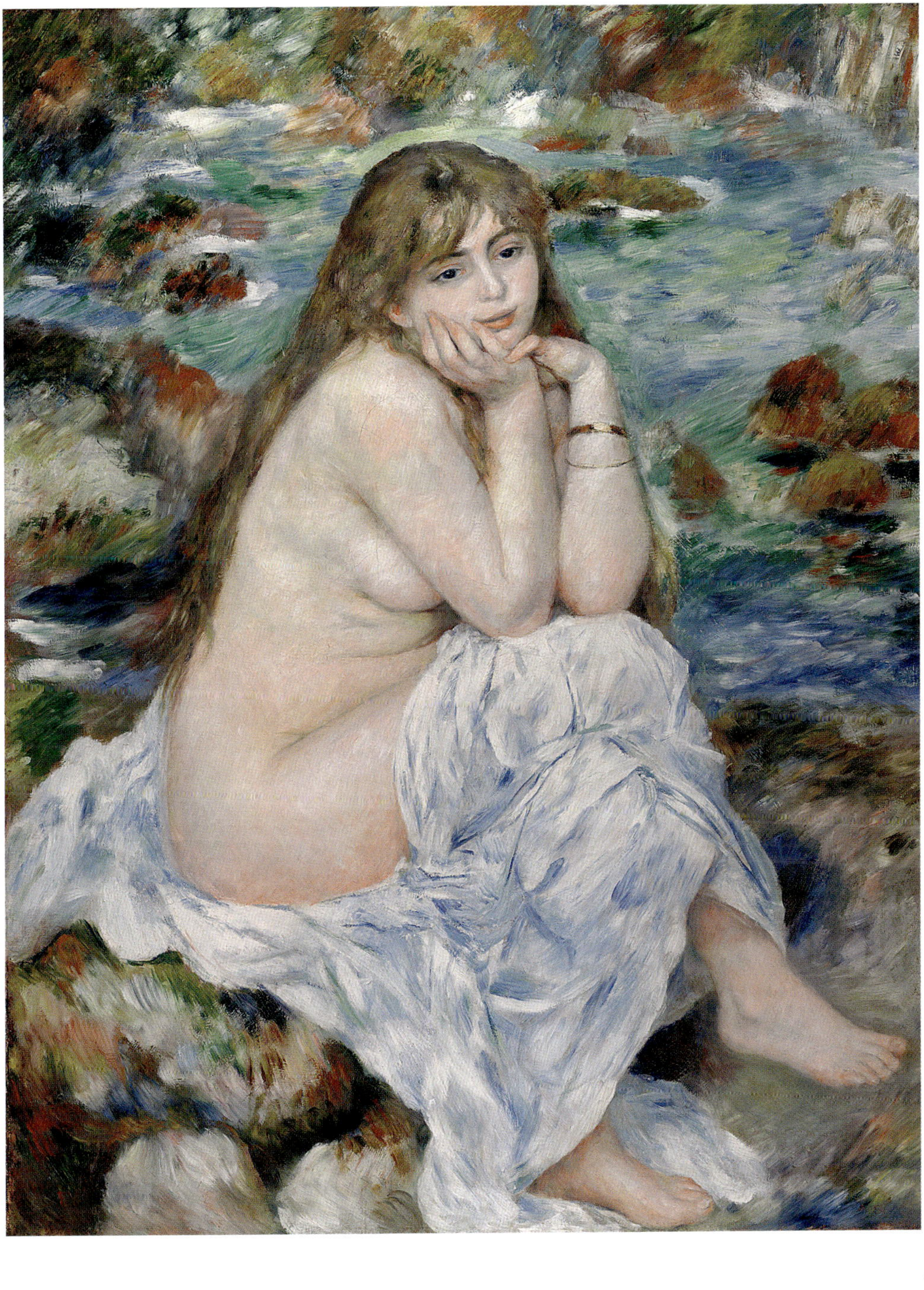

The Great Bathers, 1884–7

Oil on canvas
117.5 × 171 cm
Philadelphia Museum of Art

"Everyone today is preoccupied with painting, but these same people completely neglect an art that used to be the glory of France and doesn't exist anymore today. What I mean is decorative art." First exhibited over May and June 1887 at Georges Petit's Sixth International exposition, this picture was subtitled by the artist "Experiment in Decorative Painting". This reference was not just an overture to secure decoration commissions but a deliberate positioning of Renoir in a lineage of grand decorators from Pompeii via Raphael to French painting of the *ancien régime*.

The painting had a lengthy gestation and numerous drawings—some uncharacteristically large—attest to the care Renoir put into the arrangement and execution of this large work. Morisot visited Renoir's studio. "I saw two drawings of women going into the water, which I found as charming as any work by Ingres. He said that nudes seemed to be one of the essential forms of art." The pose of the rightmost girl is taken from François Girardon's bas-relief *Nymphs Bathing* (1668–70), which Renoir had studied carefully. He apparently drew a copy, now lost.

When first displayed, the painting received a very mixed response. Durand-Ruel, Renoir's main dealer, was firmly opposed to the new Ingresque style. It remained unsold until 1889 when it was acquired by a friend, painter Jacques Émile Blanche, for the low price of 1000 francs. *The Great Bathers* has since come to be seen as perhaps Renoir's greatest masterpiece. It is a rich, harmonious design that combines the grandeur of classical decorative art, Ingresque finish and Impressionist luminosity. The grace and beauty of the figures and interaction between the characters makes this one of Renoir's most mature and complex multifigure pictures. The three women—based on different models, each with a different hair colour—are archetypes or characters and not just animated bodies. It is to be regretted that this care about developing character in figures was necessarily sacrificed in Renoir's later periods. The emphasis on mood and effect entailed the inevitable loss of individualisation.

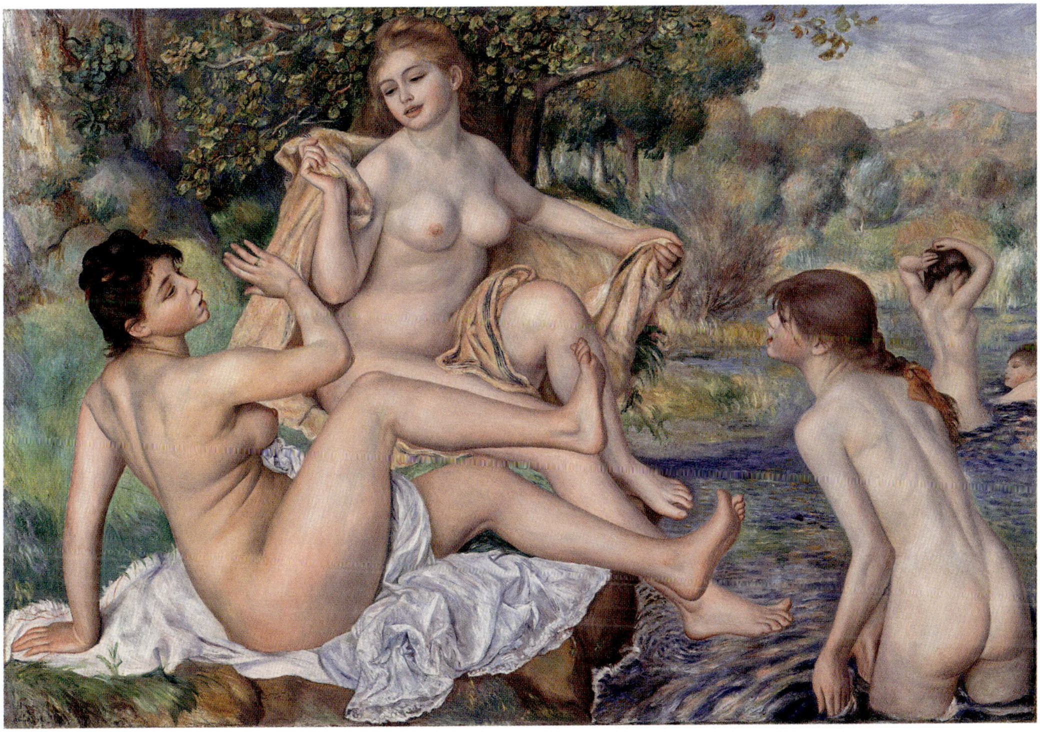

Young Girls at the Piano, 1892

Oil on canvas
116 × 90 cm
Musée d'Orsay, Paris

The subject of children and women engaged in leisure pursuits in domestic settings became synonymous with Renoir's painting. They were popular subjects for private commissions. In addition to scenes of siblings together, Renoir made pictures of mothers with children, and nannies with infants. Some pictures of peasants with children were posed for by his maids and cleaners. Domestic work at the Renoir household sometimes included posing for the master of the house.

In May 1892 the artist's friend Stephane Mallarmé and critic Claude Roger-Marx persuaded Henri Roujon—the director of the fine art museums of France—to purchase this painting for the state. It would become the first national purchase of a Renoir picture; the price paid was 4000 francs. It was only the second Impressionist painting to enter the state's collection, the first being by Sisley. Resistance to Impressionism was apparent in the initial refusal of the Caillebotte bequest (page 70).

There are three variants of this composition in oils and another in pastel. Like many artists, Renoir made multiple versions of successful designs to go to museums and private collections. He altered approaches, colours and levels of finish. In conversation, Renoir indicated that having composed a design, making changes in subsequent versions allowed him to understand the significance of form and colour in combination. Having a pre-made design freed up Renoir to explore and experiment.

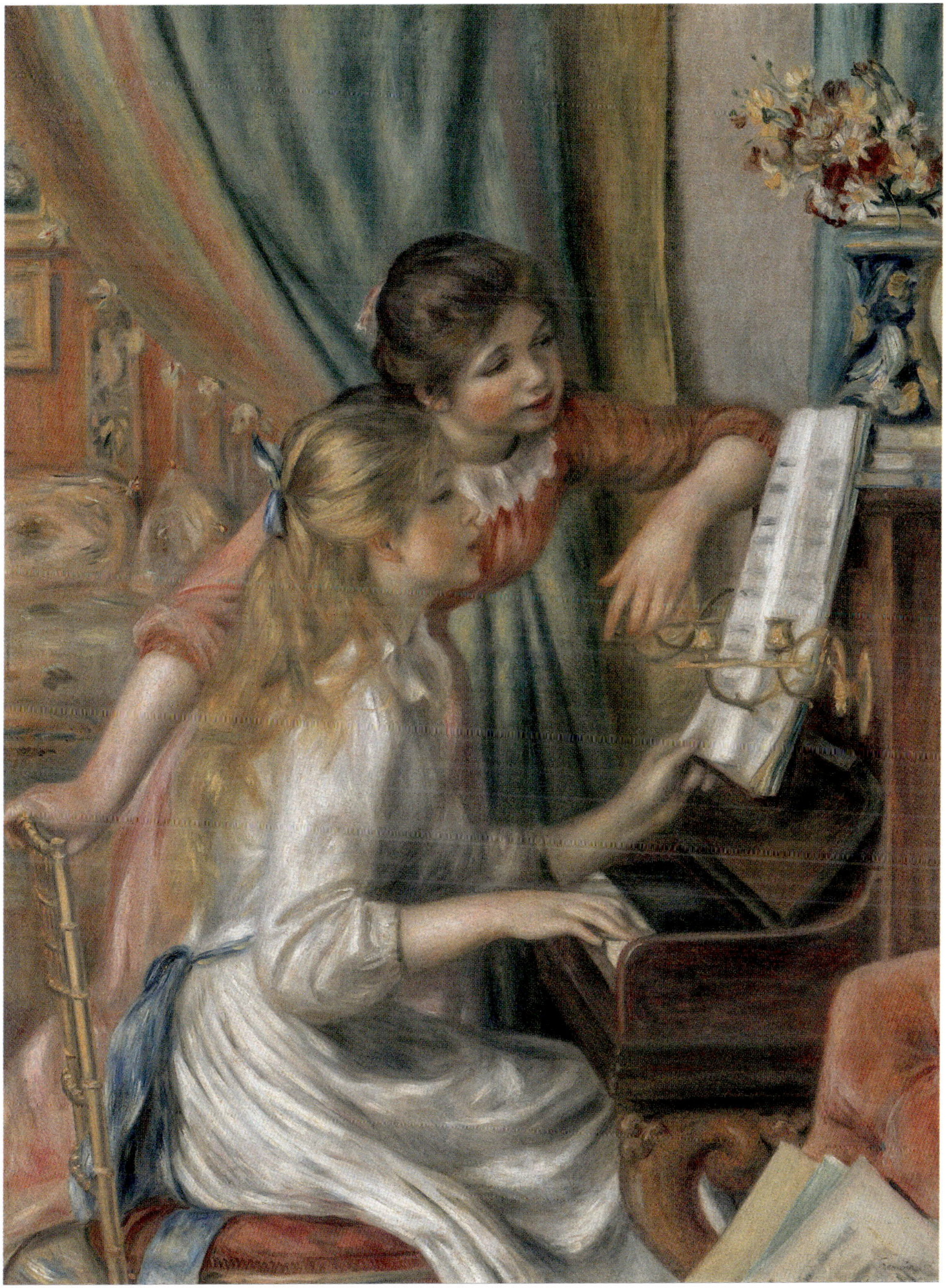

Berthe Morisot and her Daughter Julie Manet, 1894

Oil on canvas
81.3 × 65.4 cm
Private collection

Berthe Morisot (1841–1895) married Eugène Manet (brother of Édouard) in 1874. She would become a constant member of the Impressionist group. Her art "seizes wonderfully the familiar presence of a woman of the world, or a child in the pure atmosphere of the sea-shore, or green lawn", according to Mallarmé. Morisot was treated respectfully by Renoir, who took her art seriously. She would be largely responsible for organising the last Impressionist exhibition, in 1886. Renoir helped arrange a posthumous retrospective of Morisot's art.

Her daughter Julie Manet (1878–1966) would be a model for both her mother and Renoir, and later became a minor painter. Her parents died within three years of each other, leaving her an orphan, aged 16, and Renoir as her surrogate father. Her diary records the intimacy of Renoir and her family. On 4 August 1899, Julie wrote of the rapidly ageing artist, "M. Renoir's health varies from day to day, then either his feet or his hands swell; this malady is very tormenting, and he, although so highly strung, bears it with immense patience. He is cheerful, very gentle with us, and speaks in the most interesting way. What an intelligence he has! He sees clearly and correctly in everything, just as in his art".

Renoir rejected the emancipation of women. "Why teach women such boring occupations as law, medicine, science and journalism, which men excel in, when women are so fitted for a task which men can never dream of attempting, and that is to make life bearable?" Yet—as with his views on Jews—Renoir's reservations about women's equality did not prevent respect and support for Morisot as an artist. He privately undertook acts of kindness towards women painters.

Renoir's conservative outlook is further highlighted by his criticism of Jews. The Dreyfus Affair of 1894 pitted Dreyfusard liberals against anti-Dreyfusard conservatives in a division sparked by accusations of treason against Alfred Dreyfus, a French army officer. Renoir backed those critical of perceived lack of patriotism on the part of Jews, yet on a personal level the artist was polite and friendly to individual Jewish acquaintances. Renoir's antipathy towards the Dreyfusard liberal cause was something with which Cézanne, Degas and Julie Manet agreed. Monet and Pissarro took the opposite side.

Both issues indicate not anger but a fiercely instinctive rejection of liberalism, which went hand in hand with a yearning for bucolic pre-Revolutionary France. His son Jean recalled, "He had a deep respect for what was still left of the eighteenth-century way of life in France."

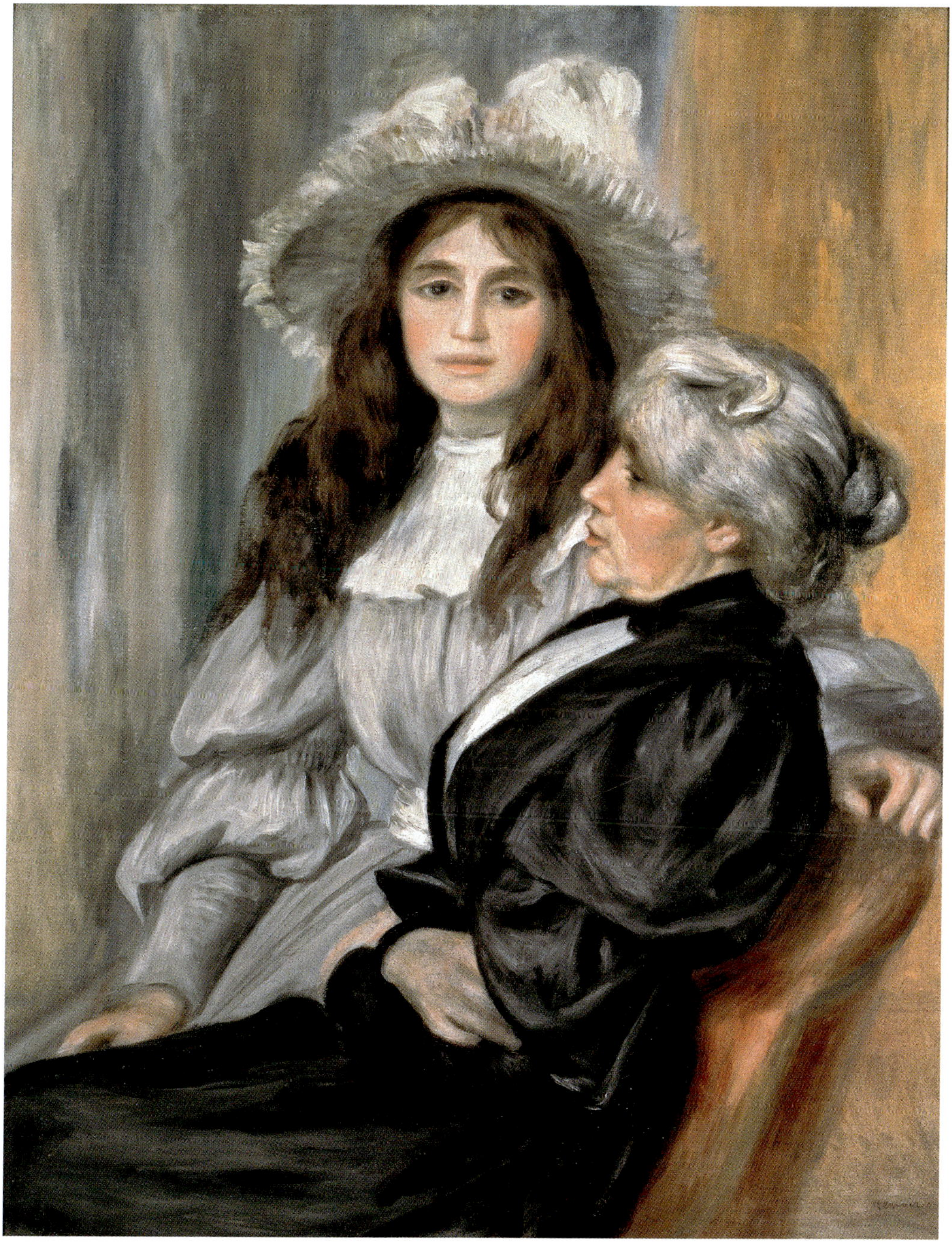

Girl Sleeping, c. 1897

Oil on canvas
82 × 66 cm
Oskar Reinhart Collection "Am Römerholz" Winterthur

One of Renoir's most alluring depictions of women, *Girl Sleeping* was painted at the end of his Pearly period. His use of colour, shade and translucent glazing conjures up the presence of the model. It was sometimes observed—and is apparent through comparison with photographs of individual subjects—that Renoir deviated from strict accuracy when painting. For him, the effect or sensation he could capture and transmit—or experience himself as he painted—was the primary concern. Often that had to be pursued at the expense of verisimilitude; indeed, the only way to achieve the effect was to invent and allow the logic of the picture to dictate forms and colours. In the Rose period, Renoir increasingly set aside accuracy in favour of idealism and invention. He painted pictures similar to *Girl Sleeping* including a lady's straw hat, where that element from everyday life tends to undermine the timeless atmosphere.
Renoir, who was dismissive of material possessions, always kept his studio spartan. "His studios, whether in Paris or in the country, are empty of any furniture that might encourage visitors to stay for long. A broken-down divan, covered in clothes and old flowered hats for his models; a few chairs that are always cluttered with canvases."
In the first book about the painter, Julius Meier-Graefe observed, "Renoir has never painted without a model, and even today there has to be one in the studio when he is working. Whether he looks at her or not is another matter". Renoir himself admitted, "The model is only there to excite me ... she allows me to try things that I would never dare invent without her". Generally, Renoir preferred to work with women he felt comfortable around. As Rivière wrote, "Sometimes he would put down his palette and gaze at them instead of painting. "Why tire yourself out?" he would say to himself. What he wanted to create existed already". The frank eroticism of Renoir's nudes has drawn some criticism from feminists but continues to appeal to viewers, both male and female, to this day.

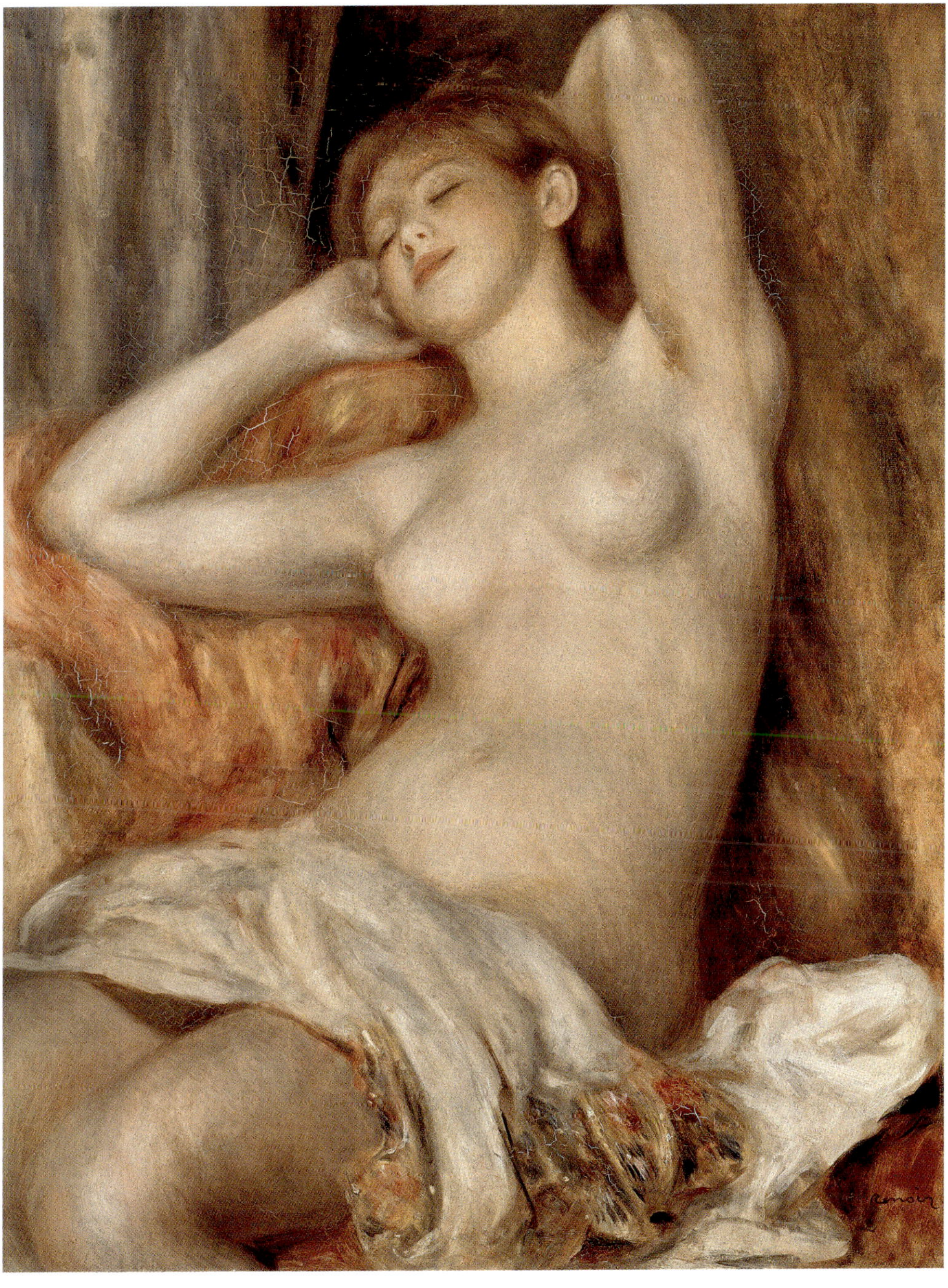

Reclining Nude (La Source), c. 1895–7

Oil on canvas
65.4 × 155.9 cm
Barnes Foundation, Philadelphia

"You feel [Roman muralists] were not striving to bring forth a masterpiece. A tradesman or a courtesan wanted a house decorated. The painter honestly tried to put a little gaiety on the wall—and that was all." However, the effort put into this picture belies that somewhat cursory outline of Renoir's.

This undated painting can be placed at the end of the Pearly period. It prefigures the Rose period, in which Renoir returned not only to a classical past but to his first love. As a student, he spent hours drawing ancient statuary in the basement of the Louvre. His Rose period is characterised by a change in palette to hot pinks, reds and orange and the adoption of the imagery and mood of ancient art. The nude was an ideal vehicle for Renoir because it is a timeless, eternal subject.

The painter's respect for decorative art is borne out by his production of decorative cast reliefs and tapestries, as well as the change in emphasis in his easel paintings, which evoke the bas-reliefs of Greece, Rome and the Rococo. Mannerist sculptor Jean Goujon and Baroque sculptor Girardon (page 92) became touchstones for Renoir of how French artists could form meaningful links back to the ancients and extend that lineage.

Reclining Nude, along with *Caryatids* (page 29), were decorative pieces that compress space and feature *trompe l'oeil* devices, such as the drapery spilling into the viewer's space out of the pictorial one. The adoption of a low viewpoint indicates the painting was to be set on a wall above head height. The painted stone frame, into which the painter has "carved" his name, acts as an intermediary device between the imaginary pictorial space and the actual architectural space. Such playful touches and blurring of boundaries are common in decorative art—ones that perfectly fitted Renoir's character and intentions.

This painting was made for collector Paul Gallimard. *Caryatids* and other decorative paintings were apparently made without a setting in mind, indicating that Renoir took such endeavours seriously and regarded them as integral to the main corpus of his art.

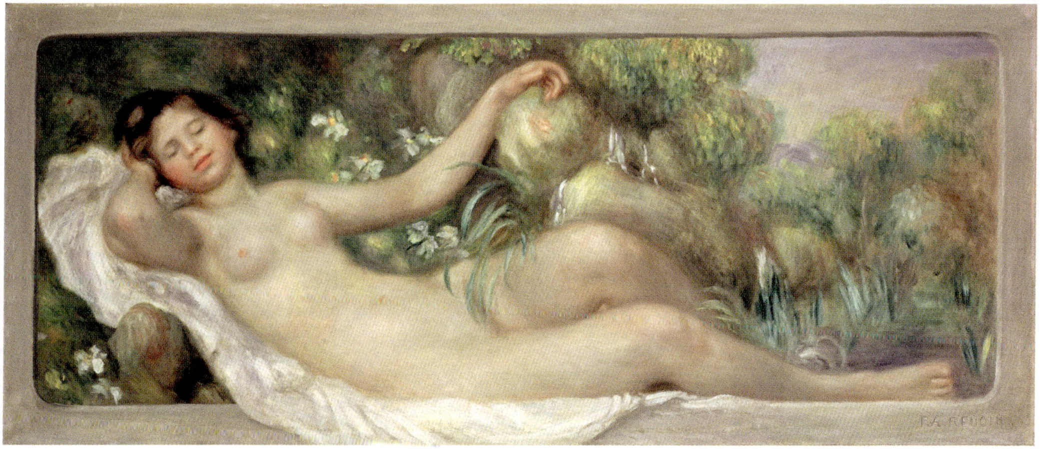

The Artist's Son, Jean Drawing, 1901

Oil on canvas
45.1 × 54.6 cm
Virginia Museum of Fine Arts, Richmond

Children, childhood and maternity became enduring themes, even before Renoir had children of his own. He displayed a serious and lively curiosity about the child sitters he depicted in portraits that, while flattering, are perceptive and original. He went beyond what was expected by a society portraitist, perhaps inspired by Velázquez, whose paintings he would see extensively firsthand in the Prado only in 1893, after he had slipped the yoke of paid portraiture.

One of Renoir's most endearing traits was his attachment to his children. Pierre, Jean and Claude (his three sons by Aline) and Jeanne (his illegitimate daughter by Lise) were very important to him. His financial support and encouragement was constant. He painted and drew his sons, from infancy onwards. Pierre would become an actor; Jean a noted film director and Claude would become a ceramicist. His daughter Jeanne would marry a baker and experience hardships, despite a posthumous annuity from her father. Jean's memoirs of his father are vivid and convey well his father's life and attitudes, with the painter's statements paraphrased from memory. Jean admitted, "Renoir would have given his life for his children without hesitation. But he was extremely reticent about revealing his private feelings to anyone—even to himself, perhaps".

"His chief desire was to bring us up among good plain things, with as few as possible of them made by machines", Jean recalled of his father. A composition of Jean and Gabrielle playing with toys was made in several versions; the version illustrated on page 27 was owned by the important collector Paul Guillaume. Guillaume acquired Impressionist, Post-Impressionist, Cubist and other School of Paris art, amassing a remarkable collection (including twenty-three Renoirs) which was acquired by the French state in 1959 and 1963. It is now housed in the Musée de l'Orangerie. Recent biographer Barbara Ehrlich White deduces that Gabrielle was probably dismissed by Madame Renoir for assisting her husband in communicating and paying money to his secret daughter Jeanne, something he concealed from the family.

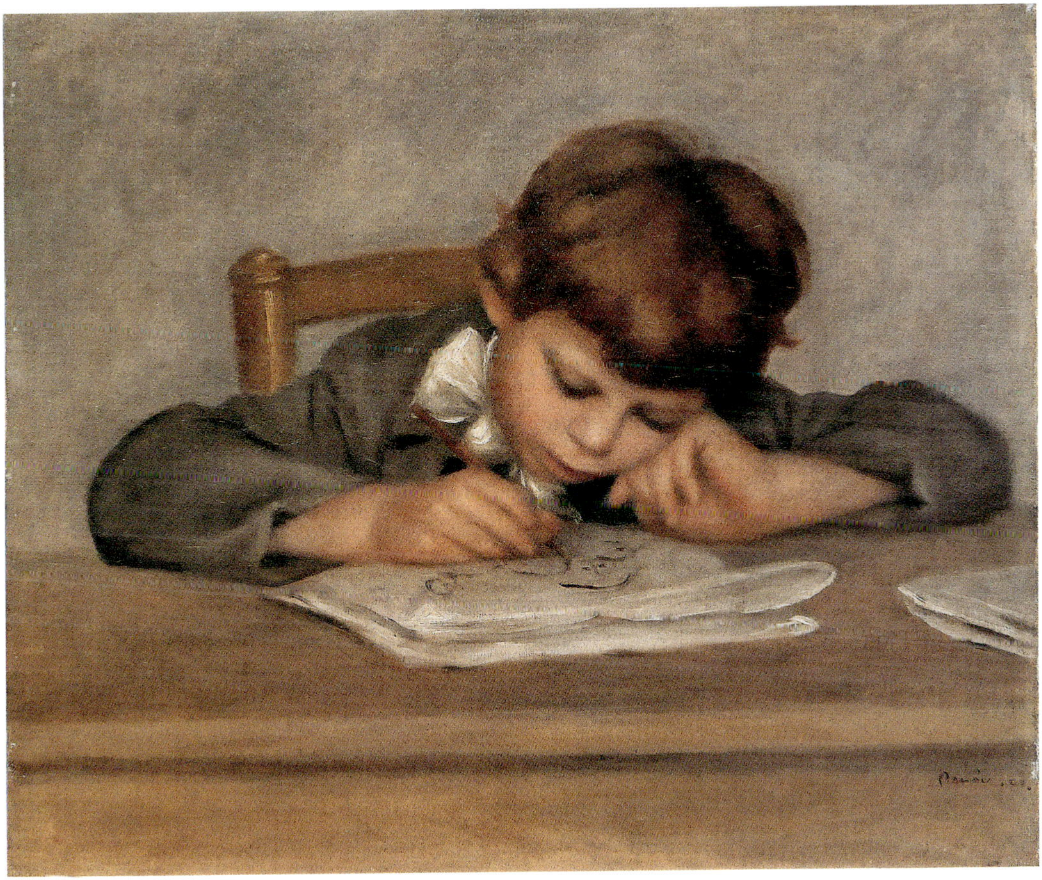

Terrace at Cagnes, 1905

Oil on canvas
46 × 55.5 cm
Artizon Museum, Tokyo

This Rose-period town view exemplifies differences between Renoir's approach in 1905 and views of Paris (page 45) from the Realist and Impressionist periods. Pink, cream, yellow and earth hues predominate; touch is light and unemphatic; reflected light seems to dissolve the solidity of the walls and roofs. The turbulent directional brushwork and passages of heavy impasto have disappeared; in their place a serene shimmer and warm diffuseness envelope us as they must have done for the artist.

The seated woman—perhaps sewing—is one among many depictions of women at leisure or engaged in genteel domestic chores. Along with Morisot, Renoir took up a subject that had been immortalised by Vermeer, other Dutch masters and Velázquez. Many of Renoir's models—both nude and clothed—came from the neighbourhoods close to his homes. Although, when portraying childcare or domestic labour, Renoir chose local working-class women, sewing was in fact considered a suitable accomplishment for women of all social levels. Like reading, writing or playing music, sewing helped to occupy the sitter and prevent her from becoming self-conscious or bored while Renoir painted her.

Renoir visited Cagnes-sur-Mer in 1905 in search of relief from his chronic arthritis, with an eye for attractive motifs. It was agreeable in climate and character. "The natives of Upper Cagnes had not yet had to sell their old houses to artists, or their properties on the hillside to the retired rich", wrote Jean. "They went from one to the other, perched on their little donkeys, unhurried, and never wearing out the animals, the land, or themselves. My father felt at home with them." In 1907 Renoir would purchase Les Collettes, a farm with an old orchard, that was rebuilt as a family home with adjoining studio. The placid scenes of the Mediterranean Sea differ from the early canvases of the turbulent English Channel, both in mood and coloration. The Midi's history of Roman and Greek settlement and the proximity of North Africa made dialogue with the ancients seem viable and natural for Renoir.

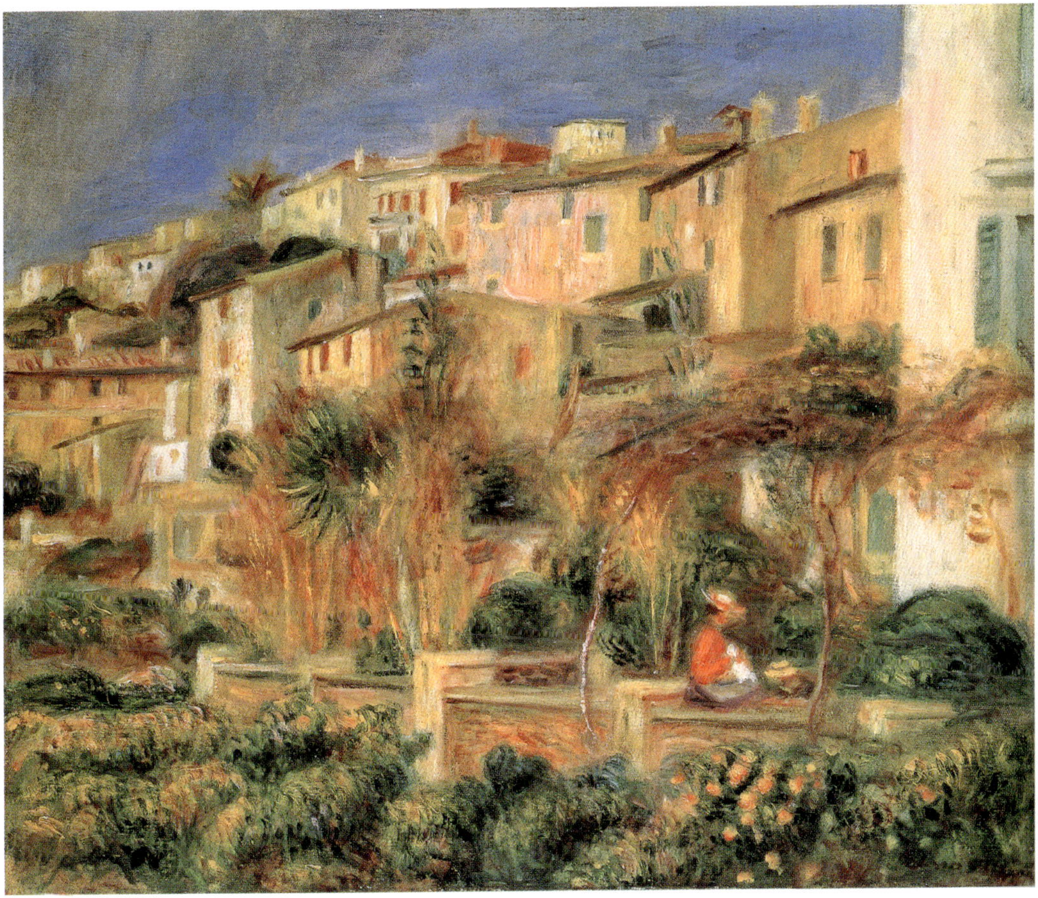

The Bathers, 1918/9

Oil on canvas
110 × 160 cm
Musée d'Orsay, Paris

This is Renoir's last major painting, finished shortly before his death and subsequently donated to France by his sons. In it we see—in the exaggerated anatomy of the model Dédée and the improvised setting—an embrace of primordial unfettered playfulness that is the wellspring of much creativity. Art here transcends physical limitations: of a crippled artist, of plausible anatomy, of actual topographic reality. It takes on a cosmic character, beyond the limits of the actual and even logical. For the late Renoir, art is a machine of pure sensation and pleasure, freed of all constraints.

In works of pure fantasy as in paintings such as *The Bathers*—by now, the model in Renoir's studio at Les Collettes was rather a subject of his imagination than a real-life one—we see Renoir take his place beside Tintoretto and El Greco. These masters of invented nude figures used anatomy in an expressive manner, freed of the obligation to follow convention. "It's because one knows how to draw that one knows how to deform", declared Renoir.

The fecund inventiveness and liberation from everything other than the artist's own expectations found in Renoir's late paintings would inspire a younger generation of artists, including Bonnard, Matisse and Picasso. Picasso's bathers and peasants of the late 1910s and early 1920s were fantasies in which anatomy was moulded like clay to convey an impression or ideal, deploying the liberated inventiveness we find in Renoir's Rose period. For both Picasso and Renoir, the ample size and weight of figures conveyed bountifulness, health and rightness. Many qualities in late Renoir's undulating surfaces and palpitating forms can be found in Pollock's paintings from the 1930s, as he straddled the threshold between figuration and abstraction.

The Bathers is pure painting, liberated from the bounds of duty and expectation—painting without a subject even. Renoir had freed himself from the task of describing a model or illustrating a tale and was absorbed in the pleasure of colour, volume and shape. In his last works, Renoir movingly reached a state of transcendence.

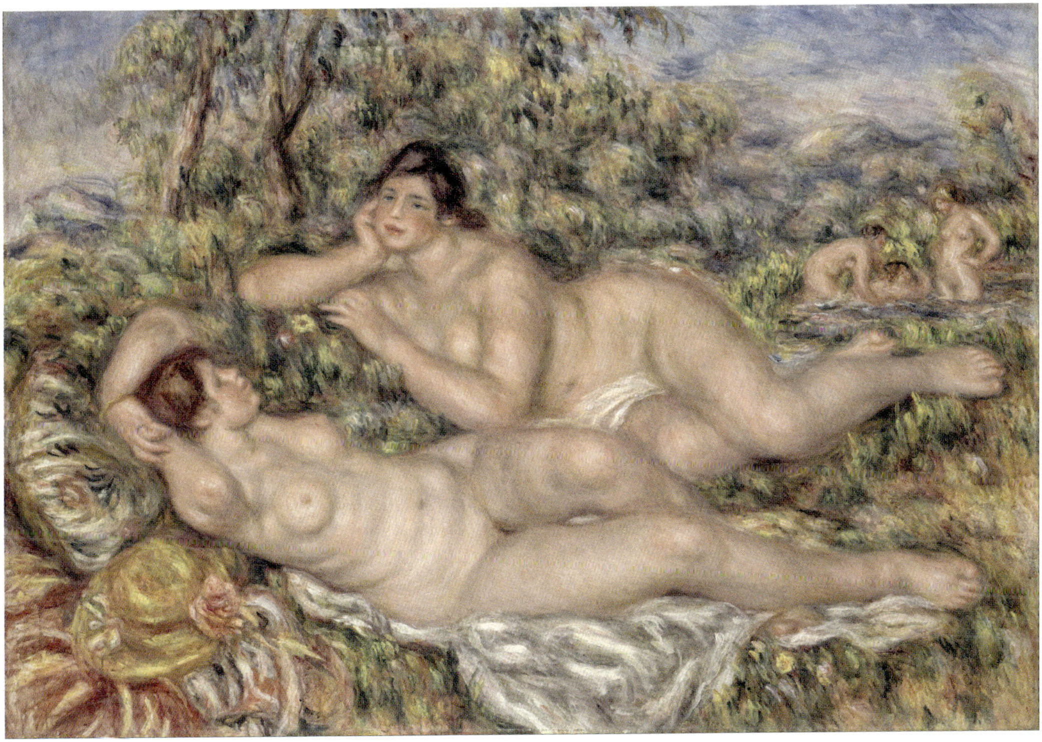

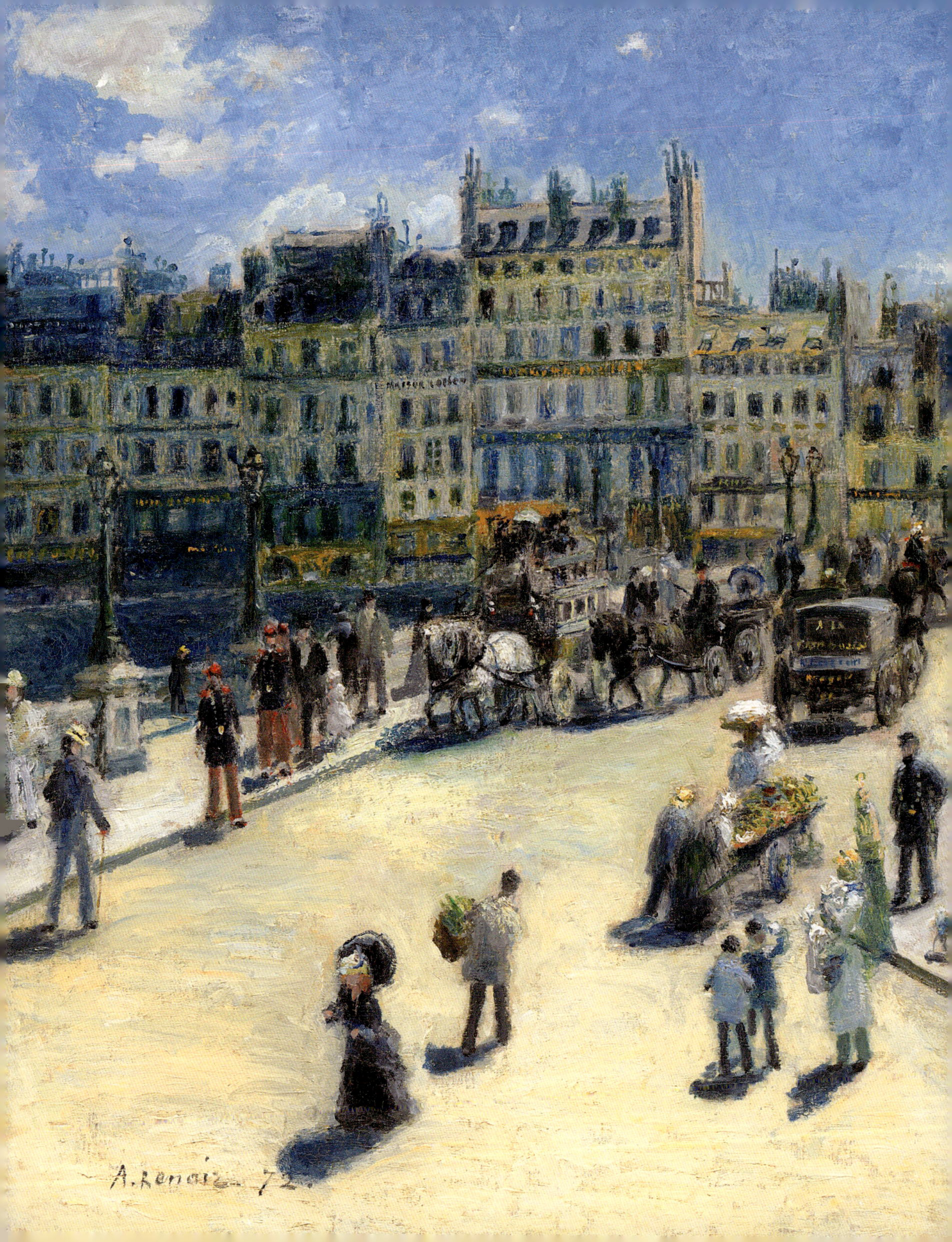
A. Renoir 72.

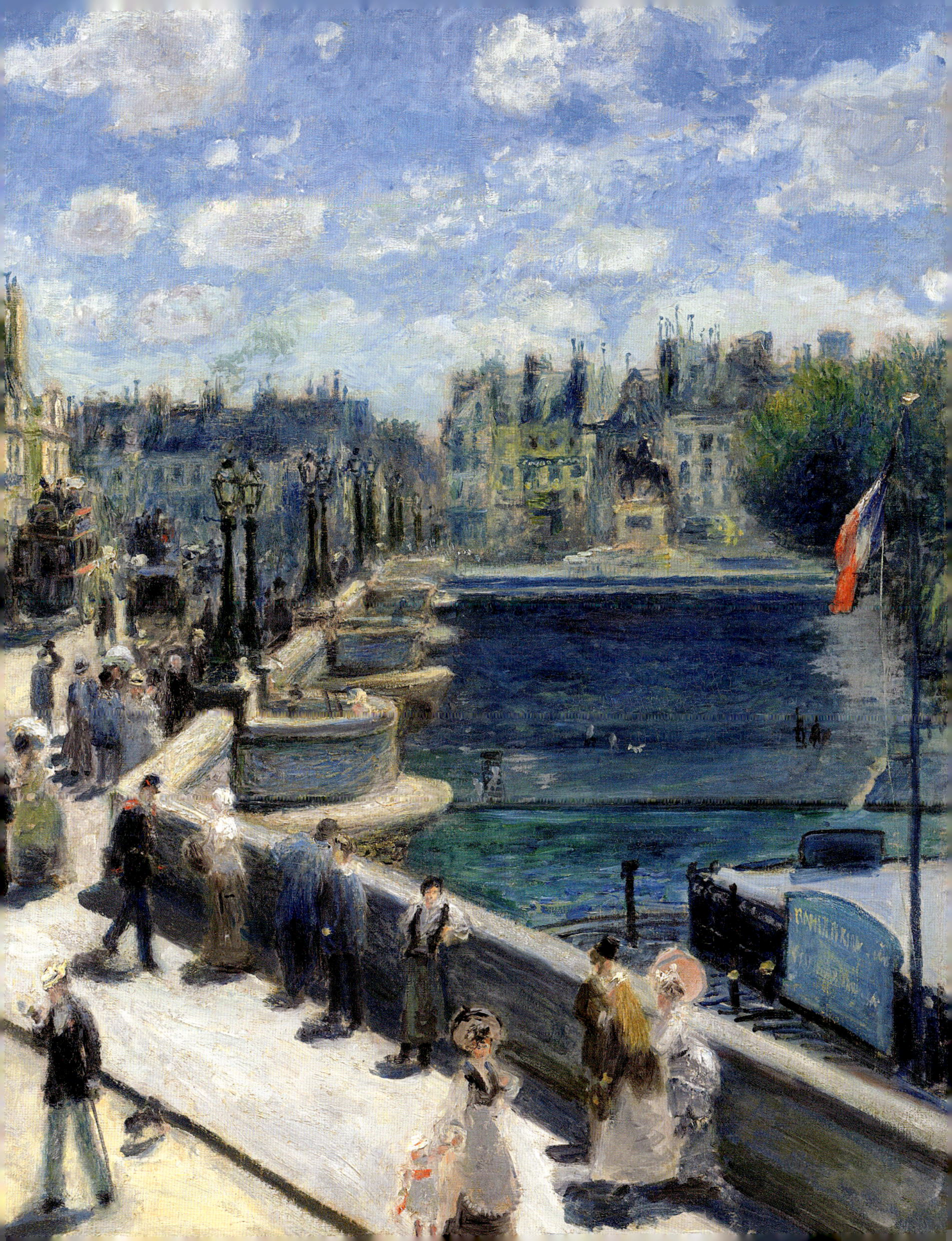

FURTHER READING

Bailey, Colin B., and Riopelle, Christopher (eds.) *Renoir Landscapes: 1865–1883*, London/New York, 2007

Bailey, Colin B., *Renoir Drawings*, New York/San Francisco, 2025

Bell, Esther, and Shackelford, George T.M. (eds.), *Renoir: The Body, The Senses*, New Haven/Williamstown, 2019

Cogeval, Guy (ed.), *Birth of Impressionism: Masterpieces from the Musée d'Orsay*, San Francisco, 2010

Denvir, Bernard (ed.), *The Impressionists at First Hand*, London/New York, 2023

Distel, Anne, *Renoir: A Sensuous Vision*, London/New York, 1995

Ehrlich White, Barbara, *Renoir: An Intimate Biography*, London/New York, 2017

Eiling Alexander (ed.), *Renoir: Rococo Revival*, Frankfurt, 2022

Fosca, François, *Renoir*, London/New York, 1964

Gaunt, William, *Renoir*, London/New York, 1982

Néret, Gilles, *Renoir*, Munich, 2025

Renoir, Jean, *Renoir, My Father*, Boston, 1962

PHOTO CREDITS

Art Institute of Chicago: 63 (Potter Palmer Collection); 75 (Mr. and Mrs. Lewis Larned Coburn Memorial Collection); 85 (Mr. and Mrs. Martin A. Ryerson Collection)

akg images: 18; 25 (akg-images/Maurice Babey); 45 (Peter van Evert)

Alamy Stock Photo: 28 (piemags/ABTB); 89 (Eraza Collection)

Artothek: 2 (IMAGNO – ARTOTHEK); 49 (Alexander Koch – ARTOTHEK); 65 (Peter Willi – ARTOTHEK); 97 (Christie's Images Ltd – ARTOTHEK)

Barnes Foundation, Philadelphia: 29 (The Barnes Foundation, BF918)

Bridgeman Images: 31, 41, 79; 24 (The Eugene and Margaret McDermott Art Fund, Inc./Bridgeman Images); 32 (© Succession Picasso/DACS, London 2026/ Bridgeman Images); 39 (© Harvard Art Museums/Bequest of Grenville L. Winthrop/Bridgeman Images); 99 (Luisa Ricciarini/Bridgeman Images); 101 (© Barnes Foundation/Bridgeman Images)

Clarke Art Institute, Williamstown: 83 (Acquired by Sterling and Francine Clark before 1955)

Fogg Museum, Harvard University: 91 (Harvard Art Museums/Fogg Museum, Bequest from the Collection of Maurice Wertheim, Class of 1906)

Metropolitan Museum of Art, New York: 17 (Catharine Lorillard Wolfe Collection, Wolfe Fund, 1907); 22 (Bequest of Julia W. Emmons, 1956)

Minneapolis Institute of Art: 81 (The John R. Van Derlip Fund)

Museo de Arte, Sao Paolo: 16 (Museo de Arte, Sao Paolo, Purchase, 1958 | Photo by João Musa)

National Gallery of Art, Washington DC: 43, 53, 67 (Chester Dale Collection); 55 (Ailsa Mellon Bruce Collection)

Philadelphia Museum of Art: 93 (The Mr. and Mrs. Carroll S. Tyson, Jr., Collection, 1963)

Sterling and Francine Clark Art Institute, Williamstown: Frontispiece (Acquired by Sterling and Francine Clark before 1955)

Wadsworth Atheneum Museum of Art, Hartford: 14/15 (Bequest of Anne Parrish Titzell)

Wikimedia Commons: Cover, 19, 20/21, 23, 27, 30, 47, 51, 59, 69, 71, 73, 77, 87, 95, 103, 105, 107 (Public Domain); 57 (Q3.P170,Q39931 Jean Pierre Dalbéra from Paris, France) (https://commons.wikimedia.org/wiki/File:La_Loge_de_P.-A._Renoir_(Fondation_Vuitton,_Paris)_(46499625955).jpg); 61 (Jean-Pierre Dalbéra from Paris, France) (https://commons.wikimedia.org/wiki/File:La_Yole_de_P.-A._Renoir_(Fondation_Vuitton,_Paris)_(46534881555).jpg)

https://creativecommons.org/licenses/by/2.0/legalcode